GOD'S WISDOM

Also by Peter C. Hodgson
from Westminster John Knox Press

Winds of the Spirit:
A Constructive Christian Theology

GOD'S WISDOM

TOWARD A THEOLOGY OF EDUCATION

Peter C. Hodgson

Westminster John Knox Press
Louisville, Kentucky

Book design by Sharon Adams
Cover design by Kevin Darst

First edition
Published by Westminster John Knox Press
Louisville, Kentucky

This book is printed on acid-free paper that meets the American National Standards Institute Z39.48 standard. ∞

PRINTED IN THE UNITED STATES OF AMERICA

99 00 01 02 03 04 05 06 07 08 — 10 9 8 7 6 5 4 3 2 1

Library of Congress Cataloging-in-Publication Data

Hodgson, Peter Crafts, 1934–
    God's wisdom : toward a theology of education / Peter C. Hodgson. — 1st ed.
        p.   cm.
    Includes bibliographical references and index.
    ISBN 0-664-25718-6 (alk. paper)
    1. Education (Christian theology)   I. Title.
    BT738.17.H63   1999
    268'.01—dc21   98-53741

CONTENTS

"Live and teach" should be a proverb as well as "live and learn." We must teach either for good or evil, and if we use our inward light as the Quaker tells us, always taking care to feed and trim it well, our teaching must in the end be for good.

—*George Eliot*

PREFACE

This book represents a new departure for me. It emerged partly out of an attempt to explain (to myself at least) certain puzzles about the educational process that have impressed themselves on me over many years of teaching. More recently I had the responsibility of coordinating a seminar on pedagogy for doctoral students in religion at Vanderbilt University, where I encountered questions about method and substance that seemed to demand theological reflection. I recognize that I am a newcomer to this discussion, and I have relied heavily on those who have contributed to it in recent years.

The primarily pneumatological framework of my proposals about "God's Wisdom" extends an emphasis already apparent in *Winds of the Spirit: A Constructive Christian Theology* (1994). Within this framework, a sharper christological focus emerged in the course of writing than I had anticipated (see chapter 4). One of the readers of the draft urged me to be even more explicit than I am about the theological particularities from whose vantage point I am glimpsing a complex human activity. Certainly each of us has access to the whole, the universal, the true—toward which the educative process in a multitude of ways draws us out from ourselves, our petty preoccupations and natural egocentrisms—only through very concrete particularities and always-risky ethical and religious commitments. I hope that the ecumenical Reformed Christian theological perspective from which I am writing will not make the book inaccessible to readers who are not necessarily Christians but who are open to considering a religious dimension of education.

A few colleagues and friends read and helpfully commented on a draft of this book: Judith Berling (Graduate Theological

Union), Edward Farley (Vanderbilt University), David Kelsey
(Yale University), and Amy Plantinga Pauw (Louisville Presby-
terian Theological Seminary). I have been able to do justice to
only some of their suggestions, which remind me of how much
I have to learn about this fascinating, inexhaustible topic. Its
very inexhaustibility reinforced my determination to say the
few things I have to say briefly. The Lilly Endowment provided
a generous research grant extending my academic leave to a full
year. I am grateful to its vice president, Craig Dykstra, and to
the director of the Wabash Center for Teaching and Learning in
Theology and Religion, Raymond Williamson, for the confi-
dence they have shown in my work. Stephanie Egnotovich, Ex-
ecutive Editor of Westminster John Knox Press, guided the
book into print in her friendly and professional way.

                                                    P.C.H.

Introduction

Teaching as a Religious Vocation

The young woman seated next to me on Southwest flight 774 looked over and struck up a conversation. She was from a rural part of Maryland, traveling to Los Angeles to visit her boyfriend. She tracks communication satellites and wondered what I do for a living. I teach in a university, I said. She paused, then smiled broadly and said with disarming sincerity, "That's wonderful! That's really wonderful." I smiled in return but didn't think to ask her why she thought it was wonderful. Later I thought to myself, yes, there really is something wonderful about it, something wondrous. How does it happen, this mysterious passage of knowledge through and between teachers and students? What awesome kind of impact does education have on people? Why is there something special, almost sacred, about the thing we call education? Is this what the young woman sensed?

I could have gone on to tell her that I teach religion and theology in a divinity school, but I have learned from experience that such a remark is likely to evoke blank stares on airplanes. Perhaps, though, she would have understood, and I regretted my lack of courage. One of the things I have done recently is to coordinate a seminar on the "teaching of religion" for doctoral students. In remarks to the class I said that the preposition "of" suggests a complex relation. Religion, we presume, is something that can be taught, something that is the *object* of teaching. We (teachers and students in a graduate program in religion) are primarily interested in the senses in which religion can be taught. But perhaps the preposition can also be construed as *subjective,* so that when we say the "teaching of religion" we mean that religion itself is something that teaches or generates an educational process. A reversal of predicates occurs; the object becomes a subject. What insight might this yield? Are there indeed religious aspects of teaching—not just the teaching of religion but teaching as such? Might teaching be conceived as a religious vocation whatever its subject—mathematics, science, art, business, humanities? Might there be such a thing as a *theology of teaching and education?* These are not questions that our seminar on teaching will pursue, I acknowledged, but I have become interested in them, and they cast a somewhat different light on our work. At this point the doctoral students were mentally scratching their heads, but perhaps the young woman would have understood.

RELIGIOUS DIMENSIONS OF TEACHING

As I began to investigate this subject, I discovered that I was not the first to have such thoughts. Apparently a widespread assumption of the ancient, medieval, and early modern worlds was that education is an essentially religious activity, with a religious object as the ultimate referent of education (truth, goodness, beauty, holiness, eternity, divinity) and a religious power or agent as the ultimate teacher (Platonic ideas, the highest good, the divine Spirit, God, Christ, Wisdom, Torah). This idea can be traced from Plato and Platonism through Clement of Alexandria, Origen, Gregory of Nyssa, Augustine, Thomas Aquinas, Calvin, and other Christian theologians. It was reformulated by Lessing and Herder in the eighteenth century and by Hegel, Kierkegaard, and Bushnell in the nineteenth. It has been present all along in the history of Judaism.

Has such an idea been abandoned in our own time? Certainly theories of education have become secularized and are now largely the province of schools of education and departments of psychology. Twentieth-century Christian theology has remained remarkably silent on the topic of education, and until recently graduate programs in religion have almost completely neglected the matter of pedagogy. Yet, surprisingly, emergent themes in modern and especially postmodern pedagogical theory may be pointing in the direction of a recovery of the religious dimension of education—themes such as education and life formation, the rhythm of education, constructive and interactive knowledge, education as the practice of freedom, connected teaching and cooperative learning. While not explicitly religious, these themes and others like them have, I believe, deeply religious and even theological implications. Some prophetic voices have been telling us for quite a while that it is so.

Alfred North Whitehead remarked in 1912 that we in the twentieth century should be content with no less than the educational ideal present from the dawn of our civilization: "The essence of education is that it be religious." A religious education inculcates duty and reverence. "Duty arises from our potential control over the course of events," while reverence perceives "that the present holds within itself the complete sum of existence, backwards and forwards, the whole amplitude of time, which is eternity."[1] What this might mean in our own context today is a major challenge. Education is no longer primarily the responsibility of religious institutions but of the state and secular corporations, and it covers every conceivable topic from cosmology to cosmetology. In the secularization and fragmentation of education, has its religious dimension disappeared?

Martin Buber concluded a famous address to an educational conference in 1926 by suggesting that the educator discovers an inner religious impulse to be in the service of the One who is able to do what human beings cannot do on their own—not only to form and transform the creation, but to *create*. Only the Spirit of God is genuinely creative; thus Buber questioned the premise of the conference theme, on "the development of the creative powers in the child." He suggested that the religious ground of education becomes more evident precisely in times of cultural fragmentation. "When all [cultural] figures are shattered, when no figure is able any more to dominate and shape the present human material, what is there left to form? Nothing but the image of God. That is the indefinable, only factual, direction of the responsible modern educator." Education, he said, is an *imitatio Dei absconditi sed non ignoti*—an "imitation of the God who is hidden but not unknown." The hidden God is known in the "in-between" of dialogical relationships, which are at the heart of education—the relationship to the "other side."[2] In this relationship, Buber suggested in a later essay, individuals will rediscover their own inner unity, which is related mysteriously to the dynamic unity of the whole, the eternal. "The educator who helps to bring human beings back to their own unity will help to put them again face to face with God."[3]

Bernard Meland, a theologian at the University of Chicago who was influenced by both Whitehead and American pragmatism, argued that the ultimate goal of education resides neither in technical information, nor in socially useful practices, nor in moral values, but in something that transcends and incorporates all of these things, a "higher goodness" that is spiritual in nature and makes of learning "an act of devotion" that relativizes all intellectual attainments. Discernment of the good beyond moral goodness requires what Meland calls the "appreciative consciousness"—a way of thinking that is reflective, imaginative, spiritual.[4]

Postmodern echoes of this theme are found in the work of the African American literary scholar bell hooks:

> To educate as the practice of freedom is a way of teaching that anyone can learn. That learning process comes easiest to those of us who teach who also believe that there is an aspect of our vocation that is sacred; who believe that our work is not merely to share information but to share in the intellectual and spiritual growth of our students. To teach in a manner that respects and cares for the souls of our students is essential if we are to provide the necessary conditions where learning can most deeply and intimately begin.[5]

In the process of teaching, we are "brought closer to the ecstatic than by most of life's experiences."[6] What this means for bell hooks is that teaching touches, evokes, energizes the very depths of the human, liberates people to realize their potential and transform the world. The power of transformation is a sacred power.

In his great work on democracy and education (1916), John Dewey touched on a principal reason for this sacral dimension by pointing out that education is an absolutely indispensable means by which human beings maintain themselves through renewal—not only the renewal of physical existence, which is necessary for all living things, but also, from one generation to the next, "the re-creation of beliefs, ideals, hopes, happiness, misery, and practices." Without education, there could be no social continuity of life, and thus no culture or civilization.[7] Dewey himself did not understand education in religious terms. But religion is concerned with those events, practices, and beliefs that form the root or boundary experiences of life, the points at which the fundamental mystery of life itself is most directly encountered. Along with birth, growth, achievement, decline, and death, education is such a root experience. Thus religion and education have always, until modern times, been closely associated. Religious institutions have engaged in educational activity, and education has been seen to have a religious basis, a sacramental quality.

Further evidence could be adduced to support Dewey's conviction. William Perry, in his well-known study of intellectual and ethical development in the college years, identified a progression of forms in which students construe their experience: from simple dualism (right and wrong, good and evil), through multiplicity and relativism, to mature commitment. The latter has a religious quality to it—Perry called it "faith" as distinguished from "simple belief"—because it entails an investment of personal responsibility and energy, an affirmation of what is one's own, a definition of one's identity, in a relative world.[8]

The seven "multiple intelligences" identified by Howard Gardner—intelligences possessed by everyone in different degrees and combinations—culminate in "interpersonal intelligence" and "intrapersonal intelligence." The latter includes much more than self-knowledge and awareness of inner moods and desires; it also includes moral insights and religious apprehensions.[9] Thus the ethical-religious dimension is recognized by this theory, but it is psychologized and personalized. The prophetic, visionary, mystical, ethical, speculative intelligence is not adequately represented here. One could argue, I believe, for an eighth intelligence, closely related to the seventh, namely "transpersonal intelligence," and such an intelligence seems to meet the tests adduced by Gardner.[10] Persons are not limited to self-knowledge and fellow-knowledge, but have an intrinsic intelligence of the whole, the world, the ultimate, values, truth. Theologically, this has been expressed as the "feeling of utter dependence" (Friedrich Schleiermacher), the "idea of the holy" (Rudolf Otto), or "ultimate concern" (Paul Tillich). This intelligence too, along with the others, must be awakened and addressed in the educational act.

"THE LORD'S WAY OF EDUCATION"

If persons have the potential for transpersonal intelligence and are able to mature toward a kind of knowing called commitment, then the whole discussion of the place of religion in education, and of the distinction between religious and theological studies, is cast into a new light. Far from having at best a marginal place in education, religion lies at the heart of the matter. Far from allowing an unproductive conflict to persist between religious and theological studies, we must see them as essential to each other. Certainly this does not justify dogmatism, indoctrination, or parochialism, but the very opposite. It calls attention not to a specific content but to a method or process, one that is liberating, opening, empowering, exploratory. The sort of theological claim I would like to make is this: *God "teaches" through the "educing," or leading-forth, of the human spirit into the widest range of its potentialities.*[11] Through the interaction of Spirit and spirit, the possible becomes actual, the ideal becomes real, truth becomes known, beauty takes shape, the good enters into practice. This is the work of God's Spirit.

"Wisdom" (*sophia*) defines the kind of Spirit that God's

Spirit is—not a possessing, displacing, controlling, or abandoning Spirit, but a persuading, educing, nurturing, communicating, teaching Spirit, acting in profound interaction with human spirit, indeed the whole cosmos.[12] Education as growth in wisdom is evoked by God's Wisdom (*sophia tou theou*), which challenges the foolishness of worldly wisdom (*sophia tou kosmou*) (1 Cor. 1:18–2:13). This kind of education, I shall argue, can be characterized by the term *paideia* (the nurture, upbringing, disciplining of a child, *pais*), which according to Werner Jaeger was the central ideal of Greek culture, designating "the formative process of the human personality."[13] *Paideia* also was used by the author of the Epistle to the Ephesians to characterize the upbringing of children, namely, "in the nurture (*paideia*) and admonition (*nouthesia*) of the Lord" (Eph. 6:4, KJV). Horace Bushnell commented that *paideia* is the "Lord's way of education" as opposed to the "ostrich nurture" (Lam. 4:3), which abandons offspring solely to the forces of nature.[14]

Our word "education" is closely related to *paideia*. To "educate," according to the *Oxford English Dictionary*, is "to bring up (young persons) from childhood, so as to form their habits, manners, intellectual and physical aptitudes." This is accomplished by leading forth or drawing out (*e-ducere*) their intrinsic capabilities, by teaching or showing them the way.

Our words "wisdom" and "teaching" are also linked through a suggestive etymology. "Wisdom" derives from an Old English root, *weid*, "to see," thus "to know"; whereas "to teach" comes from a Germanic root, *teik*, "to show," hence "to present" or "offer to view." We are enabled to see and thus to know something by having it shown or offered to view. Wisdom is an insightful seeing or envisioning of what shows or presents itself. This does not mean that wisdom is merely perception. Rather, it is a complex cognitive stance that includes apprehension and appreciation as well as critical reflection and an orientation to practice based on life experience. It incorporates what Aristotle referred to as *phronēsis*, practical reason. Wisdom is not simply a human potency but a divine gift, empowerment, presence—a divine "teaching" that effects a paideutic transformation of human beings. This is only a beginning at defining a multivalent symbol/concept (wisdom as *sophia*) to which I shall return in detail in chapter 4.

I want to explore the possibility of developing a theology of education out of the interplay of these suggestive terms, *sophia* and *paideia*. Sophia-God engenders paideia, and paideia yields life-enhancing wisdom, a wisdom that takes the form, so I shall argue, of critical thinking, heightened imagination, and liberating practice. My hunch is that some connections exist between classical theological understandings of education and postmodern theories of a transformative pedagogy, a pedagogy that emphasizes the role of the teacher as Socratic midwife, as participant in a process of constructing meaning, discovering truth, and engendering practice that transcends both teacher and students. The roots of this process in the divine creativity may paradoxically be more evident in an age of fragmentation and deconstruction.

If paideia is "the Lord's way of education," the way of God's Wisdom, and if paideia is present in the whole of education, then the distinction between religious and theological studies that has been much emphasized in recent years needs to be rethought. As Edward Farley has pointed out, theology has become ghettoized, restricted to the wisdom internal to specific communities of faith, while religious studies has relieved itself of the responsibility of addressing and assessing the wisdom of religious traditions—their reality claims, what they are serious about.[15] In contrast to this grievous division, religious studies really ought to be internalized by theology, becoming one of its curricular moments and modes of interpretation (cultural, historical, literary, sociological), while theological reflection ought to be considered an integral part of religious studies, that part that allows itself to be pressed by the claims of a religious faith.

These, in summary, are the themes to be addressed in this small book. Chapter 2 considers the idea of "God as teacher" in classical and modern theologies. Chapter 3 summarizes the primary motifs of a "transformative pedagogy." Chapter 4 establishes the link between God's Wisdom, incarnate (for Christians) in Jesus of Nazareth, and education as paideia. Chapter 5 concludes with an analysis of the role of paideia in liberal education and religious and theological studies.

God as Teacher

Classical and Modern Theologies

When we speak of "God as teacher," we are indicating that there is something primordial, mysterious, and overwhelming about the experience of teaching and the event of education. To be sure, teaching-learning is an activity that human beings engage in, but they often have a sense that something is happening over which they do not have full control; rather, teachers along with students are caught up in it, and at its best they experience something like inspiration, the presence of a transformative power. Stephen Bayne expresses it well when he says that "teachers come to know very clearly what it means to say that God is the teacher, for they puzzle over the daily miracle of the discovery of truth and wonder how it is that . . . the mind of the student seems suddenly to be flooded with light, far more than the human teachers could ever have given him. Truth seems to speak for itself when the way is clear and the ground prepared."[1] The truth that speaks for itself, that seizes and holds the mind and transforms the human being, is of *God*, in some sense *is* God, if the word "God" has any meaning at all. To say that God is our *true* teacher means that no absolute system of human beliefs is possible, no fideism, for truth always transcends what we can know and express; and therefore what is demanded of human beings is recognition of our own finitude, humility before the subject matter.[2]

This idea is very old and probably emerged toward the beginning of human educational activity, at a time when such activity was closely related to worship and involved interaction with the natural environment and its powers. The "ultimate teacher," says Gabriel Moran, is "the universe of living and nonliving things." Early humans had a deep sense of the connectedness of the universe, so that when they said, for example, that "the sea teaches us," they meant the belief that "God teaches us through the sea."[3] Nature's teaching is God's teaching. When this idea appeared in the high cultures of Israel and Greece, it had evolved beyond the stage of natural education to that of spiritual formation (which is not divorced from nature but occurs within it). Human teaching is also God's teaching.

What follows in this chapter is by no means an exhaustive history of the theology of education. Even less is it a survey of the philosophy of education. Rather, it focuses on a few principal figures and themes, especially those of importance for our own constructive efforts.

THE HEBRAIC AND HELLENIC HERITAGES: TORAH AND PAIDEIA

Two words define the cultures of Israel and Greece, words that are intrinsically pedagogical, words that made these cultures into educational enterprises: *torah* and *paideia*. These words are the antecedents of a Christian theology of education, and they are embedded in it.

The word *torah* in the everyday speech of the ancient Israelites meant instruction given by parents to their children to teach them in matters of learning and living (cf. Prov. 1:8; 4:1; 6:20; 31:26). In this respect it was close to the root sense of Greek *paideia*. "Torah" included information, advice, instruction, and the establishment of norms. It combined what Christian theology divided into law and gospel, command and promise, for Torah provides encouragement as well as demand and the benefits that accompany obedience.[4] Simply to think of Torah as "law" is clearly inadequate.

According to tradition, God revealed the Torah to Moses at Mount Sinai, and with that revelation Judaism originated as a religion. In a sense the Torah *is* Judaism, the theology of Judaism. Jacob Neusner emphasizes that the terms are synonymous, the one native, the other descriptive. Together they designate a way to the knowledge of God and to the love and service of God; they define "the worldview and way of life of holy Israel."[5] What is it about God that is made manifest in the Torah? According to Neusner it is precisely God's mind, God's rationality. "We know the mind of God through the intellection—the modes of thought, the attitudes, the ways of reasoned communication—exemplified in the Torah." Thus the Torah is the teaching of God that reveals the mind, the very being, of God. It is not only the medium and method but the message itself. The medium is language, words, which give a unique primacy to writing and documents in the history of Judaism. These words are believed to be the very words of God, and when they are put together in discourse and arguments they form the method—a method that reveals the deep structure of intellect, which is dialectical in character ("thrust and parry, challenge and response, assertion and counterassertion"). The message is simply the knowledge and the love of God through and above all other knowledges and loves.[6]

While God and human beings are joined in a common rationality, God is at the same time wholly other and an inexhaustible mystery, the mystery that is expressed in the divine Name, the Tetragrammaton (YHWH). For the medieval kabbalists, the Torah in its mystical essence is nothing other than the divine Name, and hence is dialectically identical with God. "The Holy One, blessed be He, is called the Torah."[7] The teaching of the Torah is like a speculum, or mirror, that does not reflect a visible image of God because it itself shines with the glory of God, the glory of intellect, of rationality. It was given to Moses alone among the prophets to see "through a speculum that shines"—and at Sinai, Israel became equivalent with Moses.[8] But as a speculum the Torah is not simply identical with the glory that shines through it; rather, it reflects that glory and thus takes on a mystical quality.

Precisely because of its mystical inexhaustibility, the Torah requires constant reinterpretation in new situations. It cannot be read literalistically or fundamentalistically but only through a sophisticated hermeneutic. One must interpret and extend its meaning, must be a searcher after wisdom: "Whoever studies the Torah and does not revise it is likened unto one who sows without reaping."[9] The kabbalists recognized that the secrets of the Torah could only be understood through interpretation. The supernal wisdom shines in the words of the Torah but is not reducible to them. Rather, the words are likened to garments that cover the divine light.[10] Exegesis can with the eye of the imagination see through the garments but never strip them off. Here Judaism expresses a fundamental paradox of religion: it is impossible to see God because God does not possess a material form; yet the invisible God is known through visual forms, the highest of which are purely intelligible, namely, words, images, symbols, concepts.[11] For Judaism, God appears in countless forms, among them teaching and the teacher.

The history of commentary on and interpretation of the Torah constitutes the Talmud. The later of the two Talmuds, that of Babylonia (c. 600 C.E.), includes all the prior writings and oral traditions and is the final, inclusive authority of Judaism. Not the Torah alone, but the Torah as interpreted and extended by the Talmud, is the living revelation of God to Israel.[12]

Thus Judaism takes on the character of a continual pedagogical enterprise. All adult Jews have the duty to study and interpret the Torah. In fact, the foundations were laid in the words of the Shema for mass education in Judaism: "Keep these words that I am commanding you today in your heart. Recite [or teach] them to your children and talk about [i.e., study] them when you are at home and when you are away, when you lie down and when you rise" (Deut. 6:6–7). Rabbi Israel Goldman, a pioneer in adult Jewish education, stresses that this is a democratic pedagogy, demanding a universal education. Knowledge of God is available to everyone through study; it is not, as in most ancient cultures, reserved for a privileged priesthood. The Torah was given by God in the free desert, in the open place, and is the inalienable property of every Jew.[13] The synagogue became a school of instruction, and study a mode of worship. Later, houses of study were founded, and they have continued to the present day. One of the most famous was the Freies Jüdisches Lehrhaus established by Franz Rosenzweig in Frankfurt as part of his effort to revitalize Jewish scholarship and education in the twentieth century. Martin Buber was its director from 1933 until its forced closing in 1937, and during this period it offered education as a means of spiritual resistance to the Nazis.[14]

Study of the Torah is not a purely intellectual activity but a way of being that changes one personally. Knowledge not only informs but transforms: it joins intellect and personal salvation, enlightenment and moral condition, thus echoing Socrates' insistence that knowledge is the key to virtue. Neusner says that the goal of Torah study is the attainment of *zekhut,* which is a quality of virtue marked by acts of courtesy, consideration, restraint, self-renunciation, humility, mutuality. These are virtues embodied in a special way by women, who in other respects have been marginalized in the Jewish system of learning. "*Zekhut,* the gift that, like love, can be given but not compelled, must be called the female virtue that sits atop a male system and structure." God responds to acts of *zekhut* in ways that seem to break the rules of the Torah but in fact fulfill their intention at a deeper level, which is the love of others more than oneself, and love of the Other most of all. "God in the successor-system [of Judaism] gains what the philosophical God [of the Torah] lacks, which is personality, active presence, pathos, and empathy." God responds to individual and collective acts of virtue and renunciation, according recognition and support to those who have done some remarkable deed, but not always to those who have lived strictly in accord with the Torah.[15]

God thus becomes involved in the day-to-day life of Israel on a personal level. In the earlier traditions, God was depicted as providing the definitive *teaching* through the Torah, but not so much as the active *teacher,* one who interacts with learners, providing insight and inspiration, leading them out of themselves into the divine mystery, nurturing and sustaining them along the way. With the emergence of the figure of Wisdom as a trope of God's pedagogical presence in the world, this shift of emphasis toward God the teacher is intensified. We shall take up the uniquely Jewish figure of God's Wisdom in chapter 4.

Torah had its mythical origin in the revelation of God to Moses, but it became coterminous with the whole of Judaism. In similar fashion, paideia had its origin (partly historical, partly mythical) in the practice of a single individual, Socrates (469–399 B.C.E.), but, through the influence of one of the greatest philosophers, Plato, it became coterminous with Greek and, by extension, Western culture as a whole. Socrates himself wrote nothing, but he had an enormous influence on his pupils, who wrote about him. It is clear that he possessed a powerful, unforgettable personality, was a brilliant teacher, and by his example changed the very meaning of both virtue and knowledge. He wrote nothing down "since he held that the only important thing was the relation between the word and the living [person] to which it was, at one particular moment, addressed."[16]

Socrates' mother had been a midwife, and he said that he learned from her the art of bringing something forth out of the human spirit into the world. The art he used was that of questioning, dialectic, by which he was able to draw the idea of the good, the true, the universal out of the experiential particularities of his interlocutors. He was the first to arrive clearly at the great insight that truth is brought forth by thinking, thus that it is discovered within our own subjectivity, and that subject and object are one. The Socratic principle, says Hegel, is that what is true is something that consciousness draws out of itself in a primordial act of educing, educating. Socrates led human consciousness back into itself in order to bring it to the universal, to the good. He set this universal over against the inwardness that is merely selfish and self-centered, and thus he opposed the claim of the Sophists that the human being is the measure of all things. Rather, it is spirit (or what he called soul) that is the measure of all things, and spirit is the principle of subjectivity that is both divine and human. Spirit draws individuals out of their particularity into the whole: this is its pedagogy.[17]

Thus education became for him a religious duty, a kind of

worship, for soul, or spirit, is the divine in humanity, and Socrates regarded himself as a doctor of the soul. The soul is both mind and moral reason, and the moral virtues (courage, prudence, justice, piety) are acquired by knowledge. True virtue is true knowledge, that is, knowledge of the truth, which can never be adequately defined or fully attained. The essence of education as paideia (a term that Socrates himself did not use of his teaching but that Plato applied to him) is that it enables persons to aspire toward the true aim of their lives; it is *phronēsis*, knowledge of the good, and its completion requires a whole lifetime. Paideia is the sum total of all that a human being is—his or her inner life, spiritual being, and culture.[18]

Socrates found himself in conflict with the old form of education represented by Aristophanes and the Sophists, which acculturated citizens to traditional values and discouraged critical questions. Socrates in contrast recognized no authority but that of reason. It is not that Socrates claimed to have authoritative knowledge, but rather he believed that questioning and self-examination would enable persons to make judgments of their own. Martha Nussbaum emphasizes that Socrates did not, like Plato, believe that an intellectual elite should rule. "The historical Socrates is committed to awakening each and every person to self-scrutiny. He relies on no sources of knowledge external to the beliefs of the citizens he encounters, and he regards democracy as the best of the available forms of government, though not above criticism." In Nussbaum's view, the Socratic ideal remains as relevant today as it was twenty-four hundred years ago. It is the essential foundation of liberal democracy and liberal education.[19]

Plato (c. 427–347 B.C.E.) brilliantly combined poetry and philosophy in creating a series of dialogues in which Socrates had a central role, but which expressed Plato's own ideas as he developed them into an encompassing educational system. His philosophy, says Werner Jaeger, is in essence paideia, setting forth a new pattern of reality and value that displaces the old religious foundation of culture—or rather offers itself as a new religion.[20] He begins in *Protagoras* by comparing the Sophists, who for a fee crammed people's minds indiscriminately with all sorts of external information, with Socrates, who sought the unity of all the virtues in knowledge and who inquired into the fundamental nature of knowledge and virtue. In *Gorgias* Plato moves on to a comparison of paideia with rhetoric. Rhetoric is the art of using words and language to persuade audiences, regardless of the content of what is said. Rhetoric as such is pure power, an instrument of force, war, conquest, as opposed to the nurturing, cultivating, thinking quality of paideia.

In *Meno* Plato begins to sketch the new knowledge that forms the basis of virtue and education. The *eidos*, or idea, is that through which all the separate virtues can be seen to be one and the same. In the idea, the logical universal and the ontological entity form an absolute unity. The essence and real being of virtue is the idea of virtue. Plato is an objective idealist who allows no division between being and knowing. His "idea" is, in Hegel's term, a concrete universal, combining within itself the ideal and the real. The purpose of Plato's dialectic is to make people consciously aware of the universal and to discover the one principle underlying the many, the unity of identity and difference.[21]

Plato moves on to a consideration of the union of eros and paideia in *The Symposium.* Education follows from the impulse of eros, the striving to attain the good and the beautiful, the spiritual ascent from lower to higher stages of love. Education is a process of growth, the formation of humanity out of the raw material of individuality; it is an organic process, like "a slow vegetable growth," as opposed to the individualistic methods of the Sophists. Eros for the good is the effect of the good itself as it takes shape in our souls. The good draws us toward and into itself by exercising (in Aristotelian terms) both a formal and a final causality.[22]

Plato's greatest work, *The Republic,* offers a utopian vision of a state whose core purpose and highest virtue is education.[23] At the same time, this is a religious vision, for Plato is convinced that paideia is ultimately the work of God and that devotion to it is "the service of God" (that is, worship). Plato's

God is not like the gods of earlier Greek religion, which in his view were powers that control everything in the universe, evil as well as good. Not only does that view conflict with the fundamental Socratic-Platonic conviction that human beings are responsible for their own actions, but also it is morally reprehensible and represents a mythological way of thinking. Plato's God is not so much a power as a standard: God is the good, the source of all being and knowing, the measure of all things, the perfect *paradeigma*. It is "the divine" or "divinity," not a personal power and presence. In Plato's case, the price of overcoming mythology is the substitution of a static, unchanging, lifeless measure for a living God who interacts with the world. Nonetheless, this is a form of theology, of theological humanism, for the good is an idea not in our heads but in reality, and the goal of humanity is to become godlike in virtue.

The famous allegory of the cave offers an image of paideia: just as we cannot gaze directly at the light, fire, or sun but must learn from the shadows of the world that are cast by the light, so also we cannot directly apprehend the good but only ascend to it by steps, gradually turning around from the shadows to the source, from the sensible world to the intelligible world. Thus, while the good itself is eternally unchanging, paideia is a process and a turning, a conversion, a wisdom (*phronēsis*) rooted in years of endeavor. Plato had to combat the widespread assumption that the jealousy of the gods prevents human beings from attaining theological knowledge. The Greeks could not appeal to the authority of a divine revelation as the Hebrews did, but rather only to the knowledge of the good—the good whose very nature, Plato insists, could not admit of jealousy but rather gives of itself, shares itself graciously, draws us to itself. Precisely how a standard or principle does this is not very clear.

These ideas are further refined in Plato's late work *The Laws*. God is not simply the single inexhaustible unity that is the universe, but the standard of all standards, the supreme norm. God is at the center of all legislation and education, and the cosmos is a teleological system, ruled by the supreme standard and the harmony it engenders. In this sense God is the "teacher of the whole world" (*Laws* 897b). The realm of eternal ideas is reproduced in the natural world of phenomena by the divine demiurge, and the rule of God is perfected in human consciousness through paideia. "The un-Homeric notion of God as the world's *teacher* illuminates . . . more emphatically than any other phrase the new Platonic attitude toward God."[24]

There remains some unfinished business. In *The Laws* Plato sets forth a system of elementary education intended as the paideia of the people and as the foundation of the higher education of the rulers. In this respect the elitism of *The Republic* with its emphasis on philosopher-kings is partially mitigated, but this still cannot be regarded as a genuinely democratic conception of education. It may be moving in the direction of the Socratic ideal, but Plato remains suspicious of democracy and he regards lawgivers, educators, and rulers as those who must possess the highest knowledge of God. In this work Plato develops an entire system of philosophical theology. For him there is no educational knowledge "that does not find its origin, its direction, and its aim in the knowledge of God," the two sources of which are the eternal orbits of the heavenly bodies and "the 'eternal stream of being' in us, the soul."[25] This is a conception in which God is not so much "teacher" as "teaching," a harmony, standard, ideal. God is not yet *spirit*, a dynamic, conscious, living intersubjectivity that indwells and interacts with the world and is experienced by humans as a personal presence. While the idea of "soul" is moving in this direction, Plato lacks the conceptual tools to develop it fully without reverting to the old mythology. Indeed, our own theology of education faces the challenge of finding a way to articulate the idea of God as teacher nonmythologically, that is, without thinking of God as a supernatural being who controls everything in the world and directly reveals sacred truths.

THE GREEK FATHERS:
THE ALEXANDRINES AND CAPPADOCIANS

In the Christianity of the Greek-speaking world, the classical ideal of paideia was incorporated into a way of thinking that was influenced by Hellenistic Judaism and, in particular, by the figure of Jesus Christ. For the moment we are skipping over the latter figure, to whom we shall turn in chapter 4. One of the earliest postbiblical Christian writings was the Acts of the Apostle Philip, in which the protagonist announces that he has "come to Athens in order to reveal to you the paideia of Christ." In calling Christianity the paideia of Christ, the author intended "to make Christianity appear to be a continuation of the classical Greek paideia," while at the same time the latter is "being superseded by making Christ the center of a new culture."[26]

The letter of Clement of Rome to the Corinthians (from the last decade of the first century) is a fascinating blend of Greek and Christian ideas. At the end of the letter Clement turns to the praise of paideia, thus suggesting that his epistle is a form of Christian education. Clement notes that the Septuagint (the Greek version of the Hebrew Bible) often speaks of paideia, meaning by this term the disciplining of sinners that produces a change of mind. But he especially notes the phrase *paideia tou kyriou* ("nurture of the Lord") used in the Epistle to the Ephesians (6:4), and undoubtedly he has this in mind when he speaks of the "paideia of God" or the "paideia of Christ" as the greatest force in the life of the Christian. Clement develops a comprehensive concept of the divine paideia, and in his final prayer he gives thanks to God for sending us Christ, "through whom Thou hast educated and sanctified and honored us."[27]

During the second and third centuries, pedagogical models of the redemption accomplished in Christ began to appear. These earliest atonement theories are of considerable importance to a theology of education and are considered in chapter 4. Our focus at present continues to be on the Christian appropriation of paideia, which culminated in the theologians of Alexandria and Cappadocia. Clement of Alexandria (died c. 215) and Origen (c. 185–254) made use of philosophical speculation to support a positive religion based on divine revelation and teaching as mediated through a holy book. Thus they were consciously bringing together paideia and torah under the figure of Christ.[28]

Clement of Alexandria's *Paedagogus* (*The Instructor*) is quite a remarkable work, with grandiose claims and vivid images. Clement's basic assumption is that Christ is the divine educator who transcends every other paideia. Faith fulfills the pedagogical mission of humanity to a higher degree than Greek philosophy, and the greatest achievements of the latter, such as Plato's philosophy, can be seen to have been borrowed from Moses.[29] It is appropriate, writes Clement,[30] to speak of the Word of God as the *Paedagogus*, or Instructor, because the Word invites human beings to salvation in a hortatory fashion, using persuasion and arts of healing rather than force. Just as those who are diseased in body need a physician, so those who are diseased in soul need a pedagogue to cure their souls, and then a teacher to train and guide the soul to the requisite knowledge of salvation. If the pedagogue is in the strict sense the one who leads the child (*pais*, child + *agein*, lead) to the teacher, and if Christ is the pedagogue, are we to assume that God is the ultimate teacher? This seems to be Clement's intention, although of course the one Word of God is active throughout the whole process (*Paed.* 1.1). Since "pedagogy" means the training of children, we must acknowledge that according to scripture it is *we* who are children, "the Lord's chickens" gathered under her wings (Matt. 23:37) (*Paed.* 1.5). Scripture provides many allusions to the "milk" of the Lord by which we are nourished, and this milk is also represented as the blood of Christ that we drink in the Eucharist (*Paed.* 1.6).

Clement plays freely on the image of "leading" and "guiding" in the word "pedagogue." For example, Christ our Instructor is the "helmsman" who does not yield to the winds of this world, but, "wafted on the favoring breeze of the Spirit of truth, stoutly holds on to the child's helm—his ears, I mean—until he brings him safe to anchor in the haven of heavens"(!) (*Paed.* 1.7). Clement dwells at length on the wisdom that characterizes the divine instruction, a wisdom marked by friendship, benevolence, persuasion, and consolation on the one hand, and exhortation, discipline, censure, and punishment (but never revenge) on the other. God, it seems, is just a very good teacher who is able to reap a great harvest from a tiny seed, and this points to the spirituality of the whole process (*Paed.* 1.9–12). All of this is found in Book 1 of Clement's treatise. Books 2 and 3 discuss training for Christian life in compendious detail, starting with the regulation of our bodies and eating habits: "Some men, in truth, live that they may eat. . . . But the Instructor enjoins us to eat that we may live" (*Paed.* 2.1). Very little escapes Clement's scrutiny, and he does not hesitate to state his views very frankly.

If Clement is the brilliant allegorist, Origen is the no less brilliant philosophical theologian. In his *De principiis* (*On First Principles*), paideia becomes the basis of a philosophy and theology of history. Origen regards Christianity as the greatest educational power in history. He accepts the Platonic idea that the seed of good is to be found in everything, that the cosmos is an orderly process, and that God is the pedagogue of the universe. But something is needed to transfer these sublime ideas into reality, and that something is Christ, the greatest of teachers—not a self-appointed human teacher but one who embodied the divine Logos. Although human effort is required, the divine initiative is prior. For Origen, Christ is not a single historical event but part of a continuous historical process with predecessors (prophets, philosophers, lawgivers) and successors (saints, theologians, faithful Christians). This paideutic process is the divine *pronoia*, or providence.[31]

Origen associates Christ with the Wisdom of God (*sophia*) in a suggestive way. Wisdom is the breath of the power and will of God. As such, it is the efflux of the glory of God, the rays of God's eternal life, the mirror of God's working (*De prin.* 1.2).[32] Three kinds of wisdom are encompassed within the divine providence: a wisdom of the world (poetry, grammar, rhetoric, geometry, music, medicine), a wisdom of the "princes of this world" (occult philosophies), and a wisdom of God (cf. 1 Cor. 2:6–8). When Paul refers to the latter as "secret and hidden, which God decreed before the ages for our glory," we can assume, says Origen, that this means that "it operated to a less degree in ancient and former times, and was afterwards more fully revealed and manifested through Christ" (*De prin.* 3.3). The question is how this wisdom became fully revealed in Christ. Origen employs a famous analogy: just as iron held continuously in a fire will eventually be converted into fire, so the soul placed perpetually in the Word and Wisdom of God will eventually become God in all that it does, feels, and understands (*De prin.* 2.6). Wisdom infuses and transforms the soul. This is a spiritual process, the pouring of the Holy Spirit into our hearts in such a way that we freely receive the gift of the Spirit but at the same time are inwardly changed by it (*De prin.* 2.7). Origen insists on a synergy between God's providence and human action (*De prin.* 3.1), and this synergy is at the heart of the educational process.

The Cappadocian theologians of the fourth century—Gregory Nazianzen, Basil of Caesarea, and especially Gregory of Nyssa (died c. 394)—developed a theology of education based on a high doctrine of the Holy Spirit. They insisted that the Spirit is consubstantial with the Father and the Son. By saying that the Spirit "proceeds out of" the Father and "receives from" the Son, they avoided the subordination of the Spirit to the Son that was becoming common in Western theology.[33]

Gregory of Nyssa's ideas about a Christian paideia in *De institutio Christiano* (c. 390)[34] are of great importance. He understands paideia to mean "the formative process of the human personality," and for him the key concept is "formation" (*morphōsis*). "His constant repetition of the basic image, which implies the essential identity of all educational activity and the work of the creative artist, painter, and sculptor, reveals the plastic nature of his conception of Greek paideia."[35] Human personality grows, is formed and transformed, and the ultimate transformative power is that of the Holy Spirit. This is a cooperative, not a controlling power, and Gregory had a distinctive concept of synergy: it is God who cooperates with us rather than we with God (Clement, Origen, Augustine, Luther). Believing with Plato that all humans have an eros toward the good, he says that the assistance of the divine power increases in proportion to our own effort. For Gregory it is important to put the matter this way because the Spirit is not an automatic, irresistible force. He is too deeply imbued with the Greek ideals of virtue, formation, and discipline to accept the view that human beings are passive receptors.[36] Gregory sounds almost postmodern in his insistence that students must actively participate in an educational process that is connected and relational (or "cooperative"). The teacher does not deposit information but helps to empower the student's self-learning.

For Christians the highest paideia is not philosophy but the Bible, which gives the form of Christ, and our paideutic task is to imitate Christ, that is, enable Christ to take shape within us. This formation actually occurs through the Spirit, which is "conceived as the divine educational power that is ever present in the world and that has spoken through the human beings who were its instruments." The Spirit speaks to us as the "wise educator" who neither forgets our human limits nor coerces us, but rather guides us through appropriate paideutic steps, culminating in a mystic, liberated spirituality. "What in Greek paideia had been the formation or *morphōsis* of the human personality now becomes for the Christian the *metamorphōsis* of which Paul had spoken": "Do not be conformed to this world, but be transformed by the renewing of your minds" (Rom. 12:2).[37] Again, distinctly modern themes of a transformative pedagogy seem to be anticipated by this ancient thinker.

LATIN THEOLOGY:
AUGUSTINE, AQUINAS, BONAVENTURE

Saint Augustine (354–430) touched on the theme of education as he recounted his own education in Book 1 of *The Confessions*.[38] There he described the compulsion and fear to which he was subjected as an admittedly rebellious pupil, observing that "a free curiosity has more influence in our learning . . . than a necessity full of fear" (*Conf.* 1.14). He also severely criticized the vanity, frivolity, and ineffectiveness of pagan education, which confuses things human and divine and neglects the eternal truths of God (*Conf.* 1.18).

Augustine's more extended reflections on education were

contained in his early treatise *Concerning the Teacher*,[39] which was composed in about 389 and grew out of conversations with his precocious fifteen-year-old son, Adeodatus. The central question, which harks back to Augustine's own youth, concerns the extent to which one can learn from a teacher. Teachers teach by means of words, which are signs that signify either other signs or things that are not signs. Things that are not signs are concepts that are impressed on the memory of the mind by sense experience or by inner illumination but are not produced by the sound of words. If a verbal sign (such as "head-cover") "finds me not knowing the thing of which it is the sign, it can teach me nothing" (*Teacher* 10). Thus, in the strict sense, the teacher can teach me nothing but only remind me of what I already know. How then do I know anything? Only through the truth that illumines from within, "the guardian truth within the mind itself," which is Christ, God's everlasting Wisdom, the inner teacher (*Teacher* 11). Things that we see immediately in the interior light of truth are "intelligibles," known through our own contemplation, not by the teaching of others. The most that the human teacher can do is to raise questions in such a way that the powers of the learner are brought under the direction of the inner teacher. Thus the preferred method of teaching is dialogue, and Augustine offers a dialogue between himself and his son in this treatise (*Teacher* 12).

It must be said, however, that he lacks the poetic and dialectical skill of Plato. His effort is rather heavy-handed and ends with several chapters of unbroken monologue. He tells Adeodatus, for example, that it is not the thoughts of teachers that are to be grasped by students but the sciences themselves that teachers convey through speaking. "Who is so stupidly curious as to send his son to school in order that he may learn what the teacher thinks?" (*Teacher* 14). True enough in one respect, but one wonders why this is not brought out in the dialogue between father and son rather than being laid out by the father. Augustine, who was suspicious of human teachers and ceded all authority to the Teacher in heaven, proved (in this instance at least) to have been a rather overbearing teacher himself.

Thomas Aquinas (1225–1274) directly engaged Augustine's argument, both modifying and deepening it philosophically. The principal question he addressed in question 11 ("The Teacher") of his treatise on *Truth* (*De veritate*)[40] is whether a human being or only God can teach and be called teacher (*De ver.* q.11 art.1). Supporting the position that God alone can be called teacher is not only the authority of Augustine but also Jesus' remark that "you are not to be called rabbi, for you have one teacher, and you are all students" (Matt. 23:8). However, in the very next verse Jesus also says that "you have one Father— the one in heaven," and this obviously does not mean that we have no earthly fathers. The philosophical question underlying this dispute is how humans acquire sensible forms, virtues, and scientific knowledge. Thomas embraces a middle position in accord with Aristotle: just as natural forms preexist in matter not actually but in potency and are brought to actuality by an external agent, so virtues and knowledge preexist in us in potency and are brought into activity either independently through discovery or dependently through the instruction of another. Just as the physician heals a patient through the activity of nature, so the teacher causes knowledge in a student through the activity of the latter's own natural reason. "The light of reason by which . . . principles are evident to us is implanted in us by God as a kind of reflected likeness in us of the uncreated truth." Thus, while "God alone teaches interiorly and principally," humans can teach in an exterior and secondary way. "That something is known with certainty is due to the light of reason divinely implanted within us, by which God speaks within us." Human beings do not endow the mind with the light of reason but "cooperate" with it to help it reach the perfection of knowledge. The Pauline theology of "grace" provides a biblical analogue to the Thomistic doctrine of "cooperation."[41]

The remainder of the discussion (*De ver.* q.11 arts.2–4) simply elaborates and refines this position. The whole thrust of Thomas's argument is that, while God is indeed the primary teacher, humans have a necessary secondary role to play as teachers. The reasons are partly pragmatic: a teacher who knows the whole of a science explicitly can teach it to pupils more readily than they could learn it from their own general knowledge of the principles. Moreover, teaching is an active more than a contemplative discipline. The works of mercy are part of the active life, and teaching is one of the spiritual works of mercy, namely, "teaching the ignorant the word of wisdom." The act of teaching has a twofold subject matter—the subject that is taught and the one to whom knowledge is communicated. By reason of the former, teaching pertains to the contemplative life, but by reason of the latter, to the active life. "The insight of the teacher is a source of teaching, but teaching itself consists more in the communication of the things seen than in the vision of them."[42]

By placing the emphasis on communication rather than contemplation, Thomas Aquinas is moving away from a purely mystical understanding of teaching but without destroying the mystery at the heart of education. The mystery is that the inner light of reason is implanted by God—in some sense "is" God—but at the same time is made one's own through a process of communication and reflection. God is active in the process not merely as the inner teacher but also through the agency of human teachers who evoke and explicate the potential that is present in every human being—the potential to know the truth that is God. These ideas provide a rich foundation for subsequent theologies of education.

Before moving ahead, we shall briefly consider another classic medieval text where the emphasis falls more on contemplation than communication, namely, *The Journey of the Mind to God* (*Itinerarium mentis in Deum*) by Saint Bonaventure (c. 1217–1274).[43] His basic argument is that we cannot raise ourselves to happiness, which is enjoyment of the supreme good, unless a superior power raises us. The "raising" occurs through the material universe, which is a ladder by which we may ascend to God. The highest of human powers is "synderesis," which is the natural gravity of the soul toward the good. It and the other powers are implanted in us by nature, deformed through sin, and reformed through grace. They must be cleansed by justice, trained by knowledge, and perfected by wisdom (*Itin.* 1). Through a consideration of God in vestiges in the visible world, through God's image implanted in our natural powers, and through the gifts of grace (*Itin.* 2–4), we arrive at a consideration of the divine unity through its primary name, which is *being* (*Itin.* 5). God's being comes from nothing other than itself, contains nothing of nonbeing, and thus is the being beyond all being. The contemplation of God's being comes through the light that shines upon our mind from above. Thereby we experience a spiritual and mystical transport in which all intellectual activities are relinquished and our affection passes over entirely into God, the blessed Trinity (*Itin.* 6–7). Bonaventure concludes by quoting Pseudo-Dionysius: The mysteries of theology "are shrouded in the superluminous darkness of a silence that teaches secretly in a most dark manner that is above all manifestation and resplendent above all splendor, and in which everything shines forth—a darkness which fills invisible intellects by an abundance above all plenitude with the splendors of invisible good things that are above all good."[44]

"A silence that teaches secretly in a most dark manner . . . in which everything shines forth": these mystical paradoxes sound distinctly postmodern for they have been embraced by negative theology and deconstructive philosophy. At the same time, the two elements together, communication and contemplation, point to the philosophy of Hegel, who incorporates from Thomas the necessity of mediation as well as immediacy, and from Bonaventure the images of the journey and the ladder. There are echoes here not merely of Neoplatonism but also of Jewish mysticism. This is rich material for further reflection.

REFORMED THEOLOGY:
CALVIN AND BUSHNELL

John Calvin (1509–1564), the preeminent theologian of the Reformed tradition, was no stranger to mysticism. But his was a Christ-mysticism, a "mystical union with Christ," that was influenced by Bernard of Clairvaux, rather than a cognitive or epistemological mysticism of Neoplatonic provenance.[45] Moreover, instead of speculative philosophy, Calvin employed rhetoric as a means of bringing the essentially inexpressible and unknowable God to speech.[46] Against Plato, but in line with the Latin rhetorical tradition going back to Cicero, he believed that truth is a function of persuasive efficacy, employing a panoply of images, metaphors, rhythms, and discursive breaks. The sometimes chaotic rhetorical play of Calvin's writing "opens up the possibility of readers' being grasped by a divine wisdom that can only speak to them in the fractured remains of their linguistic frameworks."[47] Calvin goes so far as to think of God, says Serene Jones, as the "Grand Rhetorician," whose word is inherently persuasive and deeply accommodating, shaped by the vicissitudes of communication. In this respect God is a masterful teacher, but what the divine teacher is, in and for godself, remains concealed behind the rhetorical play. We are led to glorify and worship God but not to probe into God's essence.[48]

One senses a Hebraic sensibility at work in Calvin's theology more than a Hellenic one. The Hebrew Bible has always had a powerful rhetorical effect on readers, and the study of the Torah by the rabbis of the Talmud was a brilliant exercise in rhetoric. The authority of the sacred writings in the life of Judaism reappears in the Protestant scripture principle, and much of Calvin's work has the character of scriptural midrash. This is true not only of his commentaries but also of his magnum opus, the *Institutes of the Christian Religion*.[49]

One way to read this work of "instruction" is to follow the steps by which Calvin moves from (human) nature as teacher, to scripture as teacher, to the Holy Spirit as teacher, to the church as teacher. In all of these, it is really God who is both the teacher and the object of teaching.

(*Human*) *nature as teacher.* Calvin believes that the knowledge of God has been naturally implanted in the minds of human beings (*Inst.* 1.3). All persons perceive that there is a God and hence have no excuse for their failure to honor God and consecrate their lives to God's will. Religion is what distinguishes human beings from the animals; the latter are capable of neither worship nor idolatry. In knowing themselves, human beings know God and vice versa (*Inst.* 1.1). Moreover, the knowledge of God shines forth in the fashioning of the universe and the governance of it (*Inst.* 1.5). The work of the Artificer is there for all to see and admire. Rather than attempting to investigate God's inner and hidden essence, we should simply "contemplate him in his works whereby he renders himself near and familiar to us, and in some manner communicates himself. . . . We need not seek him far away, seeing that he dwells by his very present power in each of us" (*Inst.* 1.5.9). But of course we fail to recognize God in nature and in ourselves for a variety of reasons: ignorance, idle speculation, vanity, idolatry, sheer malice, and sinfulness (*Inst.* 1.4). So another teacher is needed, a guide to nature and history.

Scripture as teacher. Just as those with weak vision need spectacles to read distinctly, "so scripture, gathering up the otherwise confused knowledge of God in our minds, having dispersed our dullness, clearly shows us the true God. This, therefore, is a special gift, where God, to instruct the church, not merely uses mute teachers but also opens his own most hallowed lips" (*Inst.* 1.6.1). To Calvin's legal mind, the positive law of divine teaching is needed to supplement nature's laws: the Word (of God in scripture) interprets the works (of God in nature) (*Inst.* 1.6.3). But who is to interpret the Word? What happens when the positive law is shown to be problematic or ambiguous, its lenses flawed or blurred? Calvin is not insensitive to this problem. His is not a hard doctrine of verbal inerrancy and proof-texting. Scripture is an assistance, a tool ("spectacles") that must be effectively used in rhetorically persuasive speech, and it must be confirmed by the witness of the Spirit. So yet another teacher is needed, an interpreter, a Paraclete.

The Holy Spirit as teacher. Surprisingly, Calvin does not focus in the *Institutes* on the role of Christ as teacher, although there are occasional references to him in this regard (*Inst.* 3.1.4; 3.20.1; 4.8.8). Rather, Calvin's emphasis is distinctly pneumatic.

Scripture obtains full authority among believers only when they regard it "as having sprung from heaven, as if there the living words of God were heard" (*Inst.* 1.7.1). This is a matter of seeing "as if," and believers come to see it as such through the inner witness of the Holy Spirit, which is higher than all proof, for here God speaks to us in person. The same Spirit who has spoken through the mouths of the prophets "must penetrate into our hearts to persuade us that they faithfully proclaimed what had been divinely commanded" (*Inst.* 1.7.4). The Spirit does not compel or coerce but persuades, draws, inflames us. By the power of the Spirit "we are drawn and inflamed, knowingly and willingly, to obey [God], yet also more vitally and more effectively than by mere human willing or knowing!" This is a knowledge "in which the mind truly reposes more securely and constantly than in any reasons" (*Inst.* 1.7.5). Even when it comes to the knowledge of God in Christ, we must be reminded that "no one can say 'Jesus is Lord' except by the Holy Spirit" (1 Cor. 12:3). Nothing is accomplished by preaching Christ "if the Spirit, as our inner teacher, does not show our minds the way. Only those men . . . who have heard and have been taught by the Father come to him. What kind of learning and hearing is this? Surely, where the Spirit by a wonderful and singular power forms our ears to hear and our minds to understand. . . . The way to the Kingdom of God is open only to him whose mind has been made new by the illumination of the Holy Spirit" (*Inst.* 2.2.20). Without the light of the Spirit, all is darkness; thus God gives to us "the Spirit of wisdom and revelation" (Eph. 1:17) (*Inst.* 2.2.21).

All of this is quite remarkable and, as far as I know, without precedent in the history of mainstream theology. It is Calvin who brings the Spirit onto center stage. The illumination of the Holy Spirit replaces the inner light of reason. The Spirit becomes the basis for a new epistemology and pedagogy, and even Calvin's Christ-mysticism has a pneumatic basis. Book III of the *Institutes* is concerned with the work of the Holy Spirit as the way in which we received the benefits and effects of the grace of Christ. Christ was endowed with the Holy Spirit, and

the Spirit is the bond that unites us to Christ (*Inst.* 3.1.1–2). Faith
is the principal work of the Holy Spirit. "Paul shows the Spirit
to be the inner teacher by whose effort the promise of salvation
penetrates into our minds, a promise that would otherwise
only strike the air or beat upon our ears" (*Inst.* 3.1.4). Indeed,
why does *anything* penetrate into our minds as opposed to
merely striking the air and beating upon our ears? This is the
great mystery of education. Is not the Spirit the "secret energy"
by which we learn whatever we learn, not only things of salvation but also things of the world? Teachers would teach to no
effect were it not for the "inner Schoolmaster," a metaphor
used by Calvin of both Christ and the Spirit.[50] A veil hinders us
from attaining the mysteries of God, and God's teaching is
"foolishness" to us unless it is spiritually discerned. "The Spirit
searches everything, even the depths of God" (1 Cor. 2:10). "As
we cannot come to Christ unless we be drawn by the Spirit of
God, so when we are drawn we are lifted up in mind and heart
above our understanding. For the soul, illumined by the Spirit,
takes on a new keenness, as it were, to contemplate the heavenly mysteries" (*Inst.* 3.2.34). Here the epistemological effects
of spiritually enhanced wisdom are especially clear.

The church as teacher. One more teacher is needed. The reason
seems to be that a certain structuring or ordering of the work of
the Spirit is required to resist the claim of anyone—fanatics,
tyrants, psychopaths, televangelists, white supremacists, ordinary citizens—to be inspired by the Spirit and to speak on behalf
of God. This is the function of the school, that is, of education as
an institutionalized activity, and the church is a kind of school,
the school of the Holy Spirit (*Inst.* 4.1.5). This school has persons
appointed to specific offices: apostle, prophet, evangelist, pastor,
and teacher.[51] God "forbade his people to devote themselves to
auguries, divinations, magic arts, necromancy, and other super-
stitions"—all shortcuts to saving knowledge, attempts to bypass
the lengthy pedagogical process. Thus God raised up prophets
and teachers, and it continues to be God's will to teach us
through human as opposed to supernatural means. God "provides for our weakness in that he prefers to address us in human

fashion through interpreters in order to draw us to himself, rather than to thunder at us and drive us away." God's very face "shines upon us in teaching." The Hebrews were bidden to seek the face of God in the sanctuary, for it was there that the teaching of the law and the exhortation of the prophets became "a living image of God." God revealed himself "to the holy patriarchs in the mirror of his teaching in order to be known spiritually." In other words, teaching is the speculum that shines![52]

Calvin reminds us that ministers and teachers do not displace the Holy Spirit but work through the Spirit, for they, unlike the Spirit, cannot "penetrate into minds and hearts and so correct both blindness of mind and hardness of heart" (*Inst.* 4.1.6). Teachers are to teach, not what they have "thoughtlessly fabricated," but what is contained in the law, the prophets, the apostles, and above all in the teaching of Christ. Yet since they cannot truly grasp what is contained there, "the Spirit of truth is promised to them, to guide them into a true understanding of all things" (John 16:13) (*Inst.* 4.8.8). The Spirit also operates in the sacraments, which "properly fulfill their office only when the Spirit, that inward teacher, comes to them, by whose power alone hearts are penetrated and affections moved and our souls opened for the sacraments to enter in. If the Spirit be lacking, the sacraments can accomplish nothing more in our minds than the splendor of the sun shining upon blind eyes, or a voice sounding in deaf ears" (*Inst.* 4.14.9).

These potent ideas provide the occasion for a kind of pneumatic peroration on the part of Calvin. The Spirit works in us just as a human teacher attempts to persuade students by all the pedagogical skills at his or her disposal. But the Spirit can do something no human teacher can do, namely, show us that in the sacraments "it is God speaking to us, softening the stubbornness of our heart, composing it to obedience." The Spirit completes a kind of trinitarian pedagogy: the Father of Lights illumines our minds; the Word and sacraments confirm our faith by setting before our eyes the Father's good will; while the Spirit engraves this confirmation in our minds and makes it efficacious (*Inst.* 4.14.10). We are therefore enjoined by Calvin to attend "the school of that best schoolmaster, the Holy Spirit, in which we so advance that nothing need be acquired from elsewhere" (*Inst.* 4.17.36). For this reason, education, the schooling of the Holy Spirit, is at the heart of the Reformation. Without it, nothing by way of scripture, doctrine, church, ministry, sacraments is effective; with it, in the final analysis nothing else is needed. Calvin's understanding of the role of the Spirit in the education-event represents a breakthrough on our journey toward a theology of education.[53]

We now skip ahead by three hundred years to a preeminent Reformed theologian of North America, Horace Bushnell (1802–1876). Apart from specialists in Christian education, very few modern theologians have seriously addressed the question of education. Bushnell did so partly because he was a pastor (of North Church Congregational in Hartford) and had to deal with pedagogical issues in his congregation. More specifically, however, he found it necessary to respond to a question posed by the Hartford Central Association: Are children to grow up as Christians or as converted persons? Bushnell's response took the form of two discourses on *Christian Nurture*, published in 1848. The book was republished in 1861 with fourteen additional essays and has been reissued many times since then.[54]

Bushnell takes his cue from the passage in Ephesians to which we (with his help) alluded in chapter 1, "Bring them up in the nurture (*paideia*) and admonition of the Lord" (6:4, KJV). In a manner similar to Clement of Rome, he concludes from this that "there is then some kind of nurture which is of the Lord, deriving a quality and power from him, and communicating the same." This is "the Lord's way of education," instituted by God, having a method and character peculiar to God and aims appropriate to God. In answer to the question posed to him, this means that the true idea of Christian nurture or education is "that the child is to grow up a Christian, and never know himself as being otherwise."[55]

Bushnell defended this conclusion with arguments drawn first from "the human side" and then in terms of how God might justify them. We can see from the human side, in the first place, that God's Spirit is able to work in children, who are especially "pliant to the good," as well as adults. Even adults have only *begun* to love what is good for its own sake, and they as well as children live a life mixed with good and evil. It is certainly appropriate to hold that, since the Spirit of the Lord "fills all the worlds of matter, and holds a presence of power and government in all objects, so all human souls, the infantile as well as the adult, have a nurture of the Spirit appropriate to their age and their wants."[56]

In the second place, a "law of organic connection" exists between parents and children, which means that Christian nurture is a principal responsibility of parents from the very beginning. In the "Christian scheme," the gospel is "wrapped up in the life of every Christian parent," and the faith (or lack of faith) of parents will likely be transferred to children. Children are not really born—or more strictly their character is not yet born—until they begin to emerge from the infantile state, and until then they cannot be said to have a separate nature. For many years they remain within the matrix of parental life, which continues to flow organically into them.[57]

Finally, from the human side, it is incredibly stupid and pedagogically counterproductive to bring children up with the consciousness that they are sinners who must repent and convert to the Lord at some future revival. Much of what is called Christian education only serves to make the subject of religion odious, especially when it is oriented to conversion by teaching harsh doctrine. Bushnell notes that pious parents may at the same time be very disagreeable persons and have very defective views of pedagogy, employing negative, threatening, punitive methods. The result will be sullen, silent, despairing, or rebellious children. Unfortunately, the prevailing theory of religion, says Bushnell, is that persons are to grow up in a state of evil and be dragged into the church by conquest (or as we would say, by having guilt trips laid on them). The problem, however, is not with bad children but with poor parents—parents who do not live in such a way that the light of God shines through them. Children must see that religion really is a matter of first importance to their parents, "not in words and talk, but visibly first in [their] love." It is much easier to threaten and punish children than it is to live a Christian life from which they will learn by example.[58]

The primary consideration from the divine side is that "the production of goodness is the supreme end of God," from which it may be assumed that God will bestow the grace that is necessary for the nurture of children and adults alike. The pledge of the Holy Spirit is one of God's first gifts, and it would be absurd to suppose that God "has appointed church education to produce a first crop of sin, and then a crop of holiness. God appoints nothing of which sin, and only sin, is to be the proper and legitimate result." The "Christian scheme" (one of Bushnell's suggestive metaphors for the kingdom of God) has a breadth of conception that surely recognizes the presence of sin but empowers people to struggle against it and toward redemption. A further consideration is that the organic character of humanity is recognized in scripture itself. Thus God set up families in Israel, and the Christian rite of infant baptism assumes that the child's "faith is wrapped up in the parent's faith, so that he is accounted a believer from the beginning."[59]

In a later chapter, Bushnell argues that Christian nurture is diametrically opposed to the "ostrich nurture." The ostrich "is nature's type of all unmotherhood" (cf. Lam. 4:3), for she abandons her eggs to be hatched from the warmth of the sun, and the young must go forth untended. Some people assume that human children are nurtured in the same way, simply thinking their own thoughts, generating their own principles, developing "in the freedom and beauty of the flowers." This is the approach advocated by Jean Jacques Rousseau, but Bushnell does not mention him by name. The problem with such an approach is that humans, being already touched by evil and unable to develop their minds simply by instinct, require a lengthy process of formation, cultivation, training, which is what human culture is all about. Christian virtue is "no vegetable process" but rather involves "a struggle with evil, a fall and a rescue."[60]

The question remains as to how, more precisely, God is involved in the educative process. Bushnell addresses this question indirectly in an unfinished treatise, "Inspiration by the Holy Spirit."[61] "Inspirability" is the highest human faculty, the capability of "being permeated or interiorly and receptively visited by the higher nature of God." The whole of nature is permeable by the divine omnipresence, but this entails a mere "going through" of power, whereas God's Spirit "inbreathes something of a divine quality and configures the subject in some way to itself." Human spirit is neither impenetrable nor vacuous but a "grand receptivity of life," and the Spirit of God is "to be inbreathed and interfused." The process of their interaction is called "giving understanding" or wisdom. Humans are made for God's communication, and God's very being is that of self-communication, the principal modality of which is God's "all-permeating Spirit." God's Spirit is to mind as gravity is to matter.

The implication of this theology of the Spirit for education becomes clearer when Bushnell suggests that the traditional name for the Spirit, "Paraclete," means not so much "Comforter" as "Inductor" (the "near-caller," para-clete). Education is an "e-duction" connected to the Spirit's "in-duction"; we are called/led out of ourselves by being called/led into God. This is not simply a matter of drawing out of human subjects what they already potentially know, as in Platonic recollection, but of drawing human subjects out of self-centeredness into the whole, opening them up to the universal, raising finite consciousness to the absolute, as Hegel claims.

How does the divine induction work? It cannot, says Bushnell, be understood as simply a matter of absolute divine efficiency on the one hand or of mere influence or persuasion on the other. The Spirit does operate efficiently in human subjects to prepare them for the word, convince them of sin, and raise them up to an apprehension of the divine; but there it "stops short, . . . laying no hand of force on the man that shall break his natural or thrust him out of his chosen liberty." While the Spirit is represented by material images that suggest its fluidity, permeability, and vitality, it works by "no power physically representable," and it works in the mode of immediate personal presence, although the Spirit is not literally a person. More than this cannot be said.

In his theology of the Spirit as well as his commitment to education, Bushnell stands clearly in the Reformed tradition, moving it in a more liberal direction and away from Calvinist orthodoxy, although Calvin himself and Bushnell share much in common on the themes with which we are concerned. Education is grounded in the pedagogical efficacy of the Holy Spirit, although human teachers (and parents) play a crucial role. The Spirit works as the inner teacher who invites, persuades, and (trans)forms us but does not coerce or control us. The educational task is that of drawing people out of their parochialism and self-centeredness into the wholeness that is God. Institutions such as the family, church, and school are essential to this task.

THE ENLIGHTENMENT: LESSING AND HERDER

The theology of education found in the Enlightenment philosophers Lessing and Herder shifts the focus of attention away from the education of individuals (and the institutions associated with them) to the grand scale of human history. The title of the work by Gotthold Ephraim Lessing (1729–1781), *The Education of the Human Race* (1777, 1780),[62] indicates this to be the case. In the first two propositions of this little book, Lessing establishes an identity between education and revelation: "Education is revelation coming to the individual human being; and revelation is education which has and is still coming to the human race." This means on the one hand that education is grounded in the revelatory activity of God, and on the other hand that revelation is an ongoing process of education rather than a once-for-all communication of timeless truths. As a responsible and effective teacher, God maintains a certain order, measure, and progression in revealing truths that will prove eventually to be the pure truths of reason. In this procedure the

Hebrew people have a special role to play as the teachers of other nations, but all religions contribute to the advance of humanity from infancy to maturity. Although Christ is a "better instructor," Lessing advocates a posture of tolerance toward all religions, famously so in his drama *Nathan the Wise.*

Lessing assumes the ultimate identity, not only of education and revelation, but also of reason and revelation, remarking that God "permitted and caused pure truths of reason to be taught, for a time, as truths of immediate revelation, in order to promulgate them the more rapidly, and ground them the more firmly" (§ 70). This should not be taken to imply that for Lessing talk about "revelation" is a smokescreen for an overriding rationalism that reduces God to a merely immanent principle of nature and history.[63] Rather, his position is more accurately described as a form of panentheism which affirms that all things have their being in the one God. Revealed truths become truths of reason when they are appropriated by human beings and made their own; this is what education is all about. But the truths of reason point precisely to God, who is intrinsically wise and rational.[64]

Johann Gottfried Herder (1744–1803) published in 1774 a work called *Yet Another Philosophy of History Concerning the Education of Humanity*.[65] He uses the term *Bildung* rather than Lessing's *Erziehung* (both are translated as "education" in the titles of their respective works), and by the words "yet another" he is not referring to Lessing, whose book had not yet appeared, but rather to Isaak Iselin, who had depicted history as a steady progression from superstition to Enlightenment, and to Voltaire, who saw no meaning or unity in history.[66] Against superficial optimism and unwarranted pessimism, Herder had a deep sense of the ways in which human beings have been shaped and formed (*gebildet*) by history. Human nature is not an independent entity but must learn everything, be shaped through continuous processes, and advance through gradual struggle. We are more deeply bound than we realize by our culture, time, and place, to which our views always remain relative. But it is precisely this which is an expression of divine providence, for providence requires no static universal ideal and wants to achieve its aims only through diversity and change. There is progress and development, to be sure, but it is not unidirectional and monolithic. Rather, each period has in itself the center of its own happiness, which in time becomes the foundation for a new striving. This is "the expressive pattern of God in all creation," the "theater of a guiding purpose," but none of us, being mere actors on the stage, is in a position to see it as a whole. In the history of the human race is found the "blueprint of almighty wisdom," the "painting of God," whose full meaning inevitably lies beyond the grasp of the race. From within history we can glimpse only "an unending drama with many scenes."

In a later work, *Ideas toward a Philosophy of the History of Humanity* (1784–1791),[67] Herder touches more specifically on the theme of education, arguing that humans become what they are and are able to be only through a "lifelong training toward humanity." We can speak, therefore, with Lessing of an "education of the human race," "for every individual becomes a human being only by means of education, and the whole human race lives solely within this chain of individuals." Education occurs by means of both the imitation of tradition and the exercise of our own organic powers through which we apply and reshape what has been assimilated from tradition. The latter can be called "culture" (*Cultur*) and "enlightenment" (*Aufklärung*). The goal of the educational process and the purpose of the human race is "what an individual is and can be," namely, "humanity and happiness in a specific place, to a specific degree, as a specific link, and no other, in the chain of development of the whole human race." God's purpose as the one who engenders the whole process is simply the realization and flourishing of humanity (*Humanität*) under specific temporal and historical conditions—an idea well worth remembering as we turn to our own constructive endeavor. Because God leaves the means for the formation (*Bildung*) of humanity in the hands of human beings, especially "chosen, exemplary" ones, we can expect that the path of humanity will be "shaped like a labyrinth with misleading passages on all sides," and that "every kind of vice and cruelty is exhausted in history" until nobler virtues gradually appear. When humans fail, God does not come to their rescue "through miracles but rather allow[s] these failings to produce their effects so that humans might learn to correct them on their own." That deeds have inexorable consequences is precisely a manifestation of divine providence (an idea that powerfully reappears in the novels of George Eliot).[68]

Lessing's ideas about education and revelation, and Herder's about the radical historicality of the human condition together with his understanding of the way that God's providence works through historical and educational processes toward the realization of humanity, had a powerful impact on subsequent thinkers—none more so than Hegel.[69]

SPECULATIVE AND EXISTENTIAL PHILOSOPHY: HEGEL AND KIERKEGAARD

In many respects Georg Wilhelm Friedrich Hegel (1770–1831) is to modern philosophy what Plato was to ancient: one who envisioned a new philosophical system that would encompass all aspects of reality and have a central pedagogical mission, namely, that of raising persons out of a condition of immediacy, particularity, and limited perspective to a vision of truth as the whole through a dialectical process that entails conflict, suffering, negation, and reversals. Like Plato, Hegel regarded the state as having a crucial pedagogical role, and also like Plato he regarded the whole process as having a theological provenance. The journey of the mind to God (Saint Bonaventure's image) is at the same time for Hegel the action of God, the return of God to godself. God evokes, drives, fulfills, and in some sense *is* the pedagogical process, the education-event. God is now conceived as spirit (*Geist*) rather than merely as the idea of the good: God is subject or mind as well as substance. In a manner reminiscent of the way God is known in the Torah, Hegel claims that God is intrinsically rational—rationality that is actual in and for itself as *Geist*.

In the strict (Kantian, Fichtean) sense, Hegel is not an idealist but a philosopher of spirit and an ontologist of (inter)subjectivity. He spoke of his own philosophy as "speculative" in the same sense that the Neoplatonists and the Jewish mystics spoke of "rational mystery." The mystery that is God is mirrored in consciousness, which is a *speculum* of the absolute, and a "speculative reversal" occurs between finite and infinite such that the rise of finite spirit to the absolute is at the same time the return of absolute spirit to itself. The "absoluteness" of spirit means that it is not something static and unchanging but rather intrinsically relational, having all relations internal to itself, as does the triune God.[70] Speculative philosophy is really a kind of philosophical theology.

Hegel's interest in education was already evident as a theological student at Tübingen when in 1793 he wrote an unpublished essay in which he explored the possibility that he and his rebellious friends might become enlightened religious educators (*Volkserzieher*) who would create a new folk religion (*Volksreligion*)—a religion that would accomplish in their own time what the Greeks had accomplished in theirs, namely, the integration of all aspects of life, personal, ethical, political, cultural. But Hegel already knew that this was nothing but a wistful dream, that the Greek ethos could not be restored in the modern world, and that one must come to terms with actuality as it presents itself to one's own time and place.[71]

Hegel took up the latter project full scale in his great book, *Phenomenology of Spirit* (1807), which is nothing so much as a *Bildungsroman*, a story of the formation, education, and development of the human spirit. Formative education (*Bildung*, a term that Hegel uses as a precise equivalent to the Platonic *paideia*) entails a succession of stages through which individuals are liberated from the unbroken immediacy of naive psychical life and raised to the universality of self-conscious spirit. Knowledge acquired by earlier generations through great effort sinks to the level of information, "exercises and even games for children." In this "pedagogical progress we shall recognize the history of the cultural development (*Bildung*) of the world traced, as it were, in a silhouette." Education, viewed from the side of individuals, consists in their taking inward possession of the *Bildung* that is already available to them, "making its inorganic nature organic to themselves." Looked at from the side of universal spirit as substance, what this means is that "substance gives itself the self-consciousness that properly belongs to it, brings about its own coming-to-be and reflection into itself." Thus education is the process both of individual consciousness rising to or taking possession of the universal, and of universal or absolute spirit giving itself its own self-consciousness, passing over from substance to subject. Education is at once a human and a divine process, and it is the latter not as an eternal divine standard or ideal but as a God who actualizes godself in the process.[72]

Hegel honed his pedagogical skills as rector of a *Gymnasium* in Nuremberg. When he finally took up a university appointment in Heidelberg (1816) and later in Berlin (1818), one of his goals was to write a *Staatspädagogik,* a theory of public or state-supported education, and he became acquainted with the Prussian minister of education, who brought him to Berlin. A conservative political reaction in Prussia prevented the completion of this project, however, and Hegel turned his attention to what was to become his *Philosophy of Right,* which contains several references to education.[73]

For Hegel, "education (*Pädogogik*) is the art of making human beings ethical: it considers them as natural beings and shows them how they can be reborn, and how their original nature can be transformed into a second, spiritual nature, so that this spirituality becomes habitual to them."[74] Moreover, he believed that children have the fundamental right to be educated by their parents, with the assistance of the state, and if parents fail in their responsibility the state must intervene. The state also has the responsibility of supporting the cultural and educational institutions (art, dance, music, drama, universities, scholarship) by which persons continue to be formed through their adult lives. The aim of education is to raise children out of natural immediacy to independence and free personality so that they are able to leave the family and become citizens. Spirit

consists only in making itself what it is through discipline, obedience, negation, and service.[75] It was a mistake, Hegel argued,
to withdraw children from the world, as Pestalozzi had done,
and to educate them in such a way as to allow them to pursue
only their own interests, or, as Rousseau had proposed in
Emile, to bring them up in the country in close proximity to nature.[76] Those who assume that the state of nature is innocent
will regard education as a purely external affair and a source of
corruption, but the reality is that nature is not innocent and that
education is both an inward and an outward resource for overcoming corruption.[77]

For Hegel, education requires hard labor, discipline, and
when necessary, coercion and even punishment. It involves a
transition from natural, egoistic, self-seeking will (*Willkür*) to
universal, intersubjective, free will (*freie Wille*). The former
does not yield its sway easily; it must be broken. But discipline
and coercion are negative elements; what finally pulls the self
out of its natural egocentrism is recognition by the other and,
ultimately, the summons of the absolute Other, God. Through
this process, the individual becomes a social being, and also a
political and religious one, a citizen of the state and of God's
kingdom, which is a realm of freedom. Education serves as the
means of transition from subjective spirit to objective spirit
(ethical, social, political), and thence to absolute spirit, and it is
the condition of possibility for art, religion, and philosophy.[78]
Education "is therefore *liberation* and *work* towards a higher liberation; it is the absolute transition to the infinitely subjective
substantiality of ethical life, which is no longer immediate and
natural, but spiritual and at the same time raised to the shape
of universality."[79]

Hegel also touches on the theme of education in his *Lectures
on the Philosophy of Religion* when he asks whether the knowledge
of God is an immediate or a mediated knowledge. He argues
that, on the one hand, religious knowledge is mediated: we are
educated within a religion and receive doctrinal instruction, and
positive religion is based on revelation external to the individual. But on the other hand, "neither positive revelation nor

education can bring about religion in such a way that religion would be effected from outside, something mechanically produced and placed within human beings." Mediated knowledge rather brings about a "stimulation" (*Erregung*), a "recollection" (*Erinnerung*), as Plato said, of something that we originally bear within ourselves, immediately. "Religion, right, ethics, and everything spiritual in human being is merely aroused [*erregt*]. We are implicitly spirit, for the truth lies within us and the spiritual content within us must be brought to consciousness."[80]

This has important implications for our understanding of how education actually occurs in human beings: an external stimulus brings about an internal change—both a recollection of what we know potentially and an ingestion of what has been given us, making it our own, digesting and reshaping it (rendering "its inorganic nature organic"). God's Spirit (or Wisdom) is involved on both sides of this process, witnessing to our spirits outwardly (through Christ, scripture, church, culture, revelation) as well as inwardly (through "inspiration").

Hegel's discussion of the relationship between mediated and immediate knowledge provides a convenient transition to the thought of Søren Kierkegaard (1813–1855) on our subject. In his *Philosophical Fragments*,[81] Kierkegaard imagines the possibility of moving from a strictly Socratic perspective, for which the truth is within every human being and needs only to be recollected, to its diametrical opposite, according to which human beings are in a state of utter untruth and sin. In the first instance, the teacher is of little significance, a vanishing occasion for the recollection of knowledge, a midwife, and the focus is entirely on the subjectivity of the knower. In the second instance, the learner is nothing and the teacher is everything, for the teacher must bring not only the truth but also the condition for understanding and receiving it. But no human being is capable of doing this, and so the highest relationship that can obtain between human beings is a Socratic one.

The teacher who brings the truth and the condition, and who thereby brings about a conversion and rebirth of the learner, must be a savior, a deliverer, a reconciler. This teacher could only be God. But how can the eternal, unchanging, transcendent God actually teach human beings? Only by giving up the status of divinity and becoming a human being like us. Thus, "whereas the Greek pathos focuses on recollection, the pathos of our project [the Christian project] focuses on the moment"[82]—the pathos of God's coming into existence. It really is a pathos, a suffering, for God takes on the form of a servant not as a disguise or a cloak but as a nitty-gritty reality. God "must suffer all things, endure all things, be tried in all things, hunger in the desert, thirst in the agonies, be forsaken in death, absolutely the equal of the lowliest of human beings—look, behold the man!"[83] This man is God the teacher. God teaches us, not in the glory of divinity, but in the humility and suffering of a servant, whose wisdom is foolishness in the eyes of the world. This is the paradox that is contrary to all reason and an offense to it. Acceptance of the offense is the condition for receiving the truth; Kierkegaard calls it the "happy passion" of faith by contrast with the unhappy passion of Socratic inwardness and recollection.

Kierkegaard certainly poses a stark contrast to the ways of understanding God as teacher in the mainstream of Western theology. He pushes the contrasts to the breaking point. With him it cannot be a matter of both immediate and mediated forms of knowledge, of both subjectivity and objectivity, recollection and revelation, history and God, time and eternity, particular and universal; all such "both-ands" obscure the "either/or" quality of existence, which resists ("stands out" from) systems and wholeness. Any connection between ordinary education and Christian training or practice is broken. Spiritual, mystical, and illuminationist traditions are set aside, along with the inner witness of the Spirit. The divine teaching becomes utterly miraculous, breaking ordinary cultural, pedagogical, and cognitive processes. But Kierkegaard's approach, despite its extremity, has certain advantages. It forces attention on the figure of Christ as one who incarnates and teaches a kind of wisdom that challenges the established economies of the world, and it reminds us that true education is more than recollection: it is transformation.

This last remark provides a helpful perspective from which to bring to light the hidden problematic of this chapter as a whole.[84] Christian theology does not simply graft Christ and the Holy Spirit onto an essentially unchanged Greek paideia. Paideia itself is altered in ways that are both dangerous and productive. For the Greeks there is an eros, or cognitive passion, that drives human beings to engage the real world that is already immanent within themselves, a world that is tragic in its distance from the good but not sinful, idolatrous, or deceptive. The problem is principally one of ignorance rather than illusion or false consciousness. Christianity, with its Hebraic as well as Hellenic roots, radicalizes the perception of what is wrong: there is a fall, a sinful turning away from the one true God to false gods, to idols, above all to the idol of the isolated, self-absorbed self. The remedy for this problem is not recollection but salvation, conversion, transformation. Education is not so much the drawing-forth of what the human subject already knows inwardly, but the drawing-out of the human subject from self-centeredness to God-centeredness or reality-centeredness. Christ and the Spirit play central roles in this process.

The danger in this rather subtle shift in the meaning of education is that the Greek concern with knowledge as such and as a whole—the *epistēmē* that lies at the heart of science, *scientia, Wissenschaft*—will be eclipsed by a Christian emphasis on saving knowledge, *gnōsis,* a secret wisdom given by Christ and available only to Christians in the stance of faith (Kierkegaard's "happy passion," which is an "offense" to ordinary reason). In this case, paideia has been colonized by a sectarian agenda, and the grounds have been laid for a potential conflict between paideia and *Wissenschaft* and between religious eduation and secular education (see chapter 5).

What is notable, I think, is that most of the theologians considered in this chapter, with the obvious exception of Kierkegaard, sought to avoid this rupture and to find ways of understanding how God (through Christ and/or the Spirit) is active as teacher *in congruence with* the overall process of human cultivation, not in opposition or contrast to it. There are not two truths and paideias but a single truth and paideia, at once divine and human: this is a conviction shared by the Greek and Latin theologians (notably Origen, Augustine, and Aquinas), the Enlightenment thinkers (Lessing, Herder, Hegel), and at least in principle by Calvin.

What is productive about the shift of paideia to a Christian milieu is a radicalized recognition of the tragic, fallen character of the human condition and the concomitant emphasis on *re-orientation* as well as recollection, on *transformation* as well as formation. The needed corrective to recollection is not just the Kierkegaardian pathos of the moment with its emphasis on contemporaneity with Christ, but also the Hegelian project of liberation with its orientation to the future. The achievement of human flourishing requires both a conversion and a transformation. The teacher serves as midwife to a *new,* or *second,* birth of the human being. Surprisingly, it is just this emphasis that we shall discover in several of the (ostensibly secular) pedagogies of postmodernity: the task of education is to bring about a *change of condition*—and this gives education an ethical and religious dimension.

›3‹

Transformative Pedagogy
Modern and Postmodern Theories

The history of the theology of education presented in the previous chapter came to an end in the nineteenth century. For the past hundred and fifty years, relatively little of a strictly *theological* character has been written about education *as such*. There are some important exceptions, however, and I shall consider them.[1] What was once a unitary subject (education, *paideia, Bildung*) has become compartmentalized. Nonreligious or secular theories of education are now the province of schools of education and departments of psychology and philosophy, while religious theories of education are principally the products of churches, synagogues, and schools of ministry or theology. Compartmentalization has been an inevitable consequence of both the secularization of Western culture and modern academic specialization. The latter has had beneficial effects but has also produced unfortunate consequences, such as the diminishing of pedagogical vision and the ghettoizing of theology.

In this chapter, I consider not only the religious literature but also the secular literature, with a view to finding elements within it that may point to or hint at a religious or spiritual dimension of the education-event. There has been an exponential growth in such literature since the publication of two great classics early in the twentieth century, John Dewey's *Democracy and Education* (1916) and Alfred North Whitehead's *The Aims of Education* (1929). I concentrate in this chapter on materials that have appeared during the past two decades as part of an emerging late modern or postmodern sensibility, and even here I have been very selective. Labels such as "late modern" and "postmodern"[2] are of less importance than the actual substance of what is being said, and what is being said is, I believe, of great interest.

From this recent material I have identified five principal themes of a "transformative pedagogy": (1) *education and life formation,* (2) *the rhythm of education,* (3) *constructive and interactive knowledge,* (4) *education as the practice of freedom,* and (5) *connected teaching and cooperative learning.* As I began to write this chapter, I was astonished to discover that each of these so-called late modern/postmodern themes is anticipated in one form or another by the classical and modern theologies of education I reviewed in the previous chapter. This is not to suggest that nothing has changed. On the one hand, a great deal has changed, and by finding these themes in the older literature I am bringing a contemporary interpretive lens to bear, seeing things that earlier generations might not have noticed or would have viewed differently. On the other hand, education is a very ancient human experience and a great deal of wisdom about it has accumulated through the ages. Thus I begin each of the sections that follow with a brief survey of past insights (as set forth in chapter 2) before moving into the current discussion and my own formulations.

EDUCATION AND LIFE FORMATION

The connection of education and life is one of the oldest and most persistent ideas, deriving from the primordial education human beings received (and still receive) at the hands of nature and life itself. As we have seen, Torah for the ancient Israelites meant instruction for living. It was Israel's worldview and way of life, and in this respect it has scarcely changed over three thousand years. Torah is a form of teaching, knowing, and learning that issues in personal transformation and the attainment of a distinctive kind of virtue. The same is no less true of Greek paideia, most simply defined as "the formative process of the human personality." Paideia for Socrates combined knowledge and virtue, and it enabled persons to aspire toward the true aim of their lives. It was *phronēsis*, practical wisdom, wisdom about life. Education was a process of growth, the spiritual formation of humanity, the nurture of the soul as distinct from the training of the body. Culture, politics, and religion were oriented to its service and vice versa.

These Greek ideas were incorporated by the early Christian theologians, all of whom viewed education in holistic, organic terms. Gregory of Nyssa in particular highlighted the concept of "formation" (*morphōsis*), which in Christian paideia became a "transformation" (*metamorphōsis*) of worldly standards, a reorientation to God. For Calvin education was at the heart of the Reformation and all that it had to say about scripture, church, sacraments, and the Christian life. Horace Bushnell in particular emphasized that nurture—"the Lord's way of education"—is a lifelong process, stretching from infancy to old age.

The Enlightenment philosophers expanded education onto the broad stage of history, regarding it as an ongoing process through which human beings are formed, shaped, completed. It is "lifelong training toward humanity." The youthful Hegel reveled in the Greek ideal of education as the integration of all aspects of life, and his *Phenomenology of Spirit* was the story of the formation and development of the human spirit through a process of growth, struggle, resistance, suffering, reversals, and triumphs.

For virtually all of the thinkers in the Jewish, Greek, and Christian traditions, the goal of the journey of life—the journey that constitutes Torah, paideia, *Bildung*—is identical with the source and ground of life, namely, eternal truth, the idea of the good, absolute spirit, the living God. That which calls forth education also consummates it. This latter assumption is one about which modern theorists of education have for the most part remained silent, and to which some have been openly opposed. Otherwise, however, modern understandings of the connection of education and life are remarkably consistent with long-standing views.

Of no one is this truer than John Dewey. Education, he says, is "a necessity of life."[3] Living things maintain themselves by

renewal, not only of their own lives but of their species. For human beings, this entails not only the renewal of physical existence through reproduction but also "the re-creation of beliefs,
ideals, hopes, happiness, misery, and practices." "Education,
in its broadest sense, is the means of this social continuity of
life." Above all, it is the "ineluctable facts of the birth and death
of each one of the constituent members in a social group [that]
determine the necessity of education."[4] For just this reason, it
would seem, education takes on a sacral, or religious, quality.
Religion focuses on events, beliefs, practices intimately associated with the boundary experiences and transitions of life, the
points at which the fundamental mystery of life itself is most
directly experienced, points at which the holy is encountered:
birth, natural endowment, family, cultural formation, achievement, failure and renewal, death. Education is a life-enhancing
practice. It is the means by which a newly born infant is nurtured through a laborious process into becoming a free,
responsible, thinking, acting human being; it is the means by
which persons become productive and self-supporting, and
the means by which they learn (if at all) how to grow old
and die.[5] Without it, human existence is simply inconceivable,
and thus education is a root experience of life. Dewey himself
does not pursue these religious implications, but his analysis
seems to cry out for them.

Not only are individuals dependent on education for their
very lives, but so is society. The linkage from one generation to
the next makes possible "through the transmission of ideas and
practices the constant reweaving of the social fabric." This does
not happen automatically but only through eternal vigilance.
We are always only a generation away from barbarism, and
this underscores the fragility and interdependence of culture.
Dewey recognizes that education is like art in the sense that one
has to assimilate imaginatively another's experience in order to
share one's own, but he does not recognize the religious aspect,
the fragile transmission of what Tillich calls the "substance" of
culture.[6]

According to Dewey, what enables beliefs and aspirations to

be communicated and appropriated is "the action of the environment in calling out certain responses." In other words, the
"medium" in which individuals live leads them to see and feel
one thing rather than another, to have certain plans and adopt
specific beliefs; it gradually produces in them a disposition to
take action. The words "environment" and "medium" denote
for Dewey a continuity of interactions more than physical sur-
roundings. But "environment" cannot be adequately desig-
nated as simply the "conditions" that promote or hinder the
characteristic activities of a living being. This pragmatic approach does not resolve the question of the ontological status
of environment, whether it is spiritual as well as natural,
cultural as well as social. Rather, human beings dwell in a transcendental horizon that they call "world," not just environment, and the constitution of world cannot be settled by a
pragmatic theory of knowledge.[7] Ontological and religious
questions may be bracketed, but they do not thereby disappear.
It seems rather flat to say that the ultimate source of life formation is simply "environment" or "social conditions." Nor is
it satisfactory to say that this is as far as social science can take
us, as if that disposes of the matter.

Another suggestive and recent approach to education as life
formation, including both social and intellectual formation, has
been taken by political scientist Charles W. Anderson.[8] He argues that the public purpose of the university is to initiate the
young into the way of life of a people, while its intrinsic purpose
is to find out what can be done with the powers of mind.[9] Here
he is embracing a perspective that runs from Plato and Aristotle through Kant and Hegel. With respect to both these functions—initiating into life and drawing forth the powers of
mind—education is up against a fundamental mystery. The
power of the mind is uncanny. Where and what is it? Is it strictly
an individual power that we try to draw forth, as contemporary
theories of education primarily assume? Are we just interested
in personal interpretations, feelings, views? Or is our aim to
bring students to see what all humans can see, what we can understand in common? Is the mind individual, or universal, or

somehow both? What is the "way of life of a people" into which we are initiating students? Where does it come from? Is it simply an arbitrary and contingent social product? Whence derive its values and virtues? How are we able to recognize justice and injustice when we see them? To be sure, education cannot be based on the idea of knowing universal truth directly but rather must attend to the partial, contingent, inadequate truths encountered in everyday teaching. "Yet recurrently," Anderson continues,

> during the routine process of getting an education, one should glimpse the possibility that something big is going on here, that in some respects, astonishingly, the universe is *comprehensible* and that we all do have a fundamental sense of right and wrong. One need not dwell too long in such regions. The university is really not the place to sit all day enraptured, contemplating the eternal verities. This power is better captured in sidelong glances. As natural beauty can overwhelm us only in brief doses, and then it is best to get back to hiking, or paddling, or chopping wood, so natural law and the universality of mind is something it is best to come upon, unexpectedly, in all sorts of odd places, in the course of doing other things.[10]

Here Anderson beautifully captures the religious dimension that is present in all education, especially when teachers recognize that they are initiating their students into a way of life and drawing forth the powers of their minds. I agree with Anderson that it is probably best to come upon this region unexpectedly, in the course of doing other things, and that it is unwise to dwell in it too long. But disciplined reflection on it is also necessary if education is to reach its goal, and such reflection is only caricatured if it is represented as sitting "all day enraptured, contemplating the eternal verities." There *is* such a thing as the discipline of theology, of religious studies, where what is encountered unexpectedly in odd sorts of places in other regions of study is thematized on its own account. The university *needs* this discipline if its educational purpose is to be attained.

Another aspect of education as life formation is to understand it as "growth," or "development." If life is developmental, and if developing and growing are life, then the educational implication, says Dewey, is twofold: (1) "the educational process has no end beyond itself; it is its own end"; and (2) "the educational process is one of continual reorganizing, reconstructing, transforming." Growth is not a movement toward a fixed goal; it does not have an end but is an end.

> Since in reality there is nothing to which growth is relative save more growth, there is nothing to which education is subordinate save more education. . . . The purpose of school education is to insure the continuance of education by organizing the powers that insure growth. The inclination to learn from life itself and to make the conditions of life such that all will learn in the process of living is the finest product of schooling.[11]

This comes close to making education itself a primary religious activity, one that has itself as its own end. The validity of such a view depends on what is meant by "growth." Presumably it does not simply mean "more and more," "bigger and bigger," "life for life's sake" regardless of the quality of life; but rather the enhancement of value and intensification of experience, growth in truth, beauty, goodness, wholeness, love. These latter qualities are never simply arrived at but are themselves intrinsically developing, changing, interrelating, appearing in new configurations. They point to the inexhaustible mystery of life. Life is always growing toward that mystery, and the mystery, God, is also growing. Keeping education open, growing, never finished, never exhausted by some content or dogma, helps to keep it religious.

Bernard Meland remarks that human consciousness is "a moving level of continuously creative meaning between the level of physical structures . . . and a level of good only partially and vaguely anticipated . . . toward which the human spirit, in its creative advance, is constantly bent." This is a "bent toward spirit," toward the creative ground of being, toward a higher goodness beyond the moral good, which appears in the form of love or appreciative awareness and is "a fruition of spirit which might well be called a good not our own, a beneficence that blesses relationships." The whole of human existence has access to it, and all institutions draw on its resources, but it is "higher education which fixes upon it as an object of inquiry and which assumes its nurture as a sober obligation." This makes of higher learning "an act of devotion."[12]

The theory of multiple intelligences developed by Howard Gardner also contributes to an understanding of education as life formation, for multiple intelligences are related to multiple aspects of life experience. Thomas Armstrong notes that the theory is really a philosophy of education, a multimodal model of teaching that goes back to Plato and has reappeared in Rousseau, Pestalozzi, Froebel, Montessori, and above all Dewey. There are not only linguistic intelligence and logical-mathematical intelligence, which tend to be emphasized in traditional schooling, but also spatial, bodily-kinesthetic, musical, interpersonal, and intrapersonal intelligences. The theory claims that all persons possess all intelligences, but in different combinations and capacities.[13]

It is important to emphasize that education nurtures all of these intelligences. This means, as Gabriel Moran points out, that education is broader than schools and involves family, religion, apprenticeship, employment, recreation. It is basically a lifelong process of interaction with the natural and cultural environment by which individuals grow and are transformed.[14]

All of this is important to emphasize, but something misleading and potentially dangerous also hovers about it. The emphasis on life formation can draw attention away from the necessity of critical, disciplined thinking or of what Edward Farley calls "ordered learning." Ordered learning entails the effort "to transmit by means of a sequential process of disciplined didactic activity both the insights and deposits of the past and the methods and modes of thought and work that enable new insights." Farley believes that the view of education as a total formative social process has had disastrous consequences for religious education, where the emphasis has fallen on "faith development" and virtually no ordered learning occurs. As a consequence, Sunday school is a "pseudoschool," and most believers remain at a literalist, elementary-school level in their religious understanding.[15] To some extent, this effect has invaded undergraduate college education as well: students are not acquiring the basic disciplines of thinking, speaking, reading, writing, and mathematics as well as they once did. Whether the cybernetic skills they are acquiring instead will prove to be a satisfactory substitute remains to be seen.

However, I do not believe that once education comes to mean life formation ordered learning inevitably or necessarily disappears. This might be the case if life formation were all that there is to education, but it is not. There are several other essential elements of a transformative pedagogy, one of which is precisely disciplined, critical thinking. It is especially important to emphasize that such thinking has been a critical component of paideia from the beginning, and thus I am concerned by David Kelsey's discovery that deep tensions exist today between the "Athens" model of paideia and the "Berlin" model of *Wissenschaft* (critical, disciplined knowledge, or "science").[16] Tensions arise when it is assumed that paideia is not academically rigorous or that *Wissenschaft* excludes personal engagement with the subject matter. Education is in fact a multimodal phenomenon that works best when all of its modes are in productive interplay. It is easy to allow one or more of them to slip away so that education is worn down to a simplistic, one-dimensional thing.

THE RHYTHM OF EDUCATION

That education occurs rhythmically, moving through distinct stages or cycles, is also a very old idea. It is embedded in the Socratic dialectic and in the Platonic dialogues. Through the art of questioning, Socrates was able to draw insight into the good, the true, the universal out of the experienced particularities of his interlocutors. His conversations as re-created by

Plato moved through rounds of false starts, partial refine-
ments, and gradually deepening awareness. Plato himself was
aware that education is an organic process, like "a slow vegetable growth," a maturing and ripening that goes through distinct stages and requires many, many years for its completion
(at about age fifty!). Unfortunately, from Plato's elitist point of
view, only a few gifted individuals are able to attain the highest stage, that of a philosophical priesthood.[17]

Both Augustine and Thomas Aquinas made use of the dialectical method of teaching, and Thomas elevated it to a high
art. Typically his investigation of a disputed question starts
with a thesis and supporting evidence (only God should be
called teacher because . . .), to which is opposed a counterthe-
sis (without human teachers there would be no actual education), and finally a resolution of the apparent contradiction
(God alone teaches interiorly and principally while humans
teach in an exterior and secondary way). The dialectic moves
from one-sided and limited perspectives to a more balanced
and inclusive one, which, however, leads in turn to a new question. Such is the rhythm of education.

Above all, it was Hegel who refined the dialectical method
and made it into an encompassing philosophical pedagogy.
His basic assumption was that the structure of life and thought,
of being and knowing, is one and the same. If we follow the
flow of an argument or assertion, we can see that it brings three
elements into play: (1) universality, the universal substance or
principle of a statement; (2) particularity, the particular quality
or determinate modification of the universal in the case at
hand; and (3) individuality or singularity, the subject about
which the statement makes a new predication.[18] In a similar
fashion, consciousness grows from an initial phase of immediacy through a differentiation of experience to a reintegration in
which it becomes more aware of both the unity and diversity
of reality. Consciousness comes to know itself by knowing another consciousness and then the connection between the two.
Life itself is a process that moves through the phases of identity, difference, and mediation, or of unity, separation, and rec-

onciliation. This is how change, growth, and development occur. Hegel insists that this is an unfinished, ever-changing process. It is not merely a circular one, in which things eternally return to the same point of origin, nor is it a linear process, in which one thing simply follows another. Rather, it has the character of a spiral or rhythm in which advance toward novelty occurs through the infinitely varying repetition of patterns or cycles. In making each dialectical round, one does not return to the same starting point but has moved to a new point, having gained something by way of insight into the complexity and inexhaustibility of experience. Only God is the whole, but the wholeness of God is itself a dialectical wholeness in which every conceivable diversity is encompassed.

Alfred North Whitehead acknowledges the influence of Hegel on his own formulation of "the rhythm of education."[19] By "rhythmic" he means "the conveyance of difference within a framework of repetition." Mental growth cycles repeatedly through three distinct stages, which Whitehead names "romance" (discovery, direct experience, Hegel's "immediacy"), "precision" (disciplined knowledge, mastery of technique, Hegel's "differentiation"), and "generalization" (fruition, synthesis, freedom, Hegel's "reintegration" or "mediation"). Education should consist of a continual repetition of these cycles in each unit of study, but the cycles also mark the advance of persons from infancy into adulthood.

Romance is the stage of first apprehension, when subject matter has the vividness of novelty, unexplored connections, and wealth of material. It occurs principally in the stage of early adolescence (ages eight to thirteen), when a rich world crowds into the child's life and basic skills in language and arithmetic are acquired, but education will go stale if the leaven of romance and the excitement of discovery are lost. Precision comes at the time of secondary education (ages thirteen to eighteen), when mastery of language is acquired along with precision in the basic tools of science. Generalization is the goal of university education. It should presuppose the particulars and start with general ideas, studying their application to concrete cases. The student should attain a "wide sweep of generality," which is not abstracted from concrete fact but rather appears in the form of what Hegel calls "concrete universals." Rather than cramming students with details, a university education should yield a construction and comprehension of basic principles together with a thorough grounding in the way they apply to a variety of concrete details. The principles will be remembered while the details are forgotten. Whitehead emphasizes that these stages are not simply successive; rather, they are interwoven at each stage, with one or another predominating but with the others also present. Thus at the stage of generalization it is necessary to revisit elements of precision and romance at higher levels of intellectual maturation.

The goal of this entire process, according to Whitehead, is the cultivation of mental power, which has the quality of wisdom, insight derived from principles and enriched by concrete application. A principle that has been thoroughly absorbed becomes a mental habit, which enables the mind to react in appropriate ways to various stimuli and situations. Whitehead believes that modern education has retreated from the quest for wisdom and ideals. "The drop from the divine wisdom, which was the goal of the ancients, to text-book knowledge of subjects, which is achieved by the moderns, marks an educational failure, sustained through the ages."[20] The acquisition of knowledge requires discipline; and knowledge, when mastered and appropriately employed to add value to experience, becomes wisdom, a wisdom that issues in freedom (both intimate, personal freedom and the freedom of relationships). "Freedom and discipline are the two essentials of education." Whitehead believes that they interact in a rhythmic fashion, each issuing in the other: discipline is the result of free choice, and freedom as an enrichment of possibilities is the result of discipline. "The dominant note of education at its beginning and at its end is freedom, but . . . there is an intermediate stage of discipline with freedom in subordination." The initial stage of freedom is what Whitehead calls "romance," its final stage is "generalization" or "wisdom," while the intermediate stage of discipline is "precision." He emphasizes that "there is not one unique threefold cy-cle of freedom, discipline, and freedom," but rather that "all mental development is composed of such cycles, and of cycles of such cycles."[21]

What drives this process around and forward? There seems to be a creative impulse toward growth that comes from within each individual. Children *want* to grow up. They are drawn and driven by curiosity, interest, imagination, wonder, enjoy-ment. This eros for education arises out of a spontaneous interaction with the environment and issues in a sapiential freedom. If romance is aborted prematurely, or if the process gets stuck in discipline and never arrives at freedom, then the goal of education is not attained and the adventure of life has been lost.[22]

As I understand it, this entire cyclic, rhythmic process is what constitutes paideia in the sense of the formation of human personality. It is important to stress that paideia includes the el-ement of disciplined, critical thinking as well as the element of imagination and wonder, and that the two come together to form a kind of thinking called "wisdom," which construes the wholeness of things, their "being" or "truth," and learns how to apply principles of value and goodness in concrete situa-tions. Human wisdom is evoked, empowered, and sustained by the divine wisdom, whose pedagogy is paideia: so I argue in the next chapter. The rhythmic elements of this paideia are critical thinking, heightened imagination, and liberating prac-tice. We start with naive imagination or fantasy, and move through a disciplining of thought and a maturing of imagina-tion toward a wisdom, or *phronēsis,* that grasps (though in a mirror, dimly) the ideals of truth and freedom and strives for their actualization in transformative praxis.

Another approach to the question of rhythm is taken by Mary Elizabeth Mullino Moore, whose book, *Teaching from the Heart: Theology and Educational Method,* is one of the few recent attempts at constructing a theology of education. Moore com-bines Whiteheadian process philosophy with gestalt method to form an "integrative" approach to teaching. She identifies three major elements. First, students should be given the opportunity to experience the many—the great diversity of cultural expressions, the multiple forms of reflection, the details in which ultimate truth is hidden. Second, they should be empowered to seek unity, to search for a whole that is greater than the sum of the parts. This is not a preformed whole but one that emerges through insights and patterns that present themselves in experience. Third, students should be helped to preserve the complexity of detail. In the desire to avoid the triviality of chaos, we should not settle for a trivial harmony. The goal, in Whitehead's famous formulation, is to convert oppositions and contradictions into contrasts, not to eliminate them. The complexity of contrast holds identity and diversity in balance and allows for the intensest kind of experience. Moore believes that these three elements suggest a rhythmic approach, leading from details to unification to a complexity that forces us back into more details and a new search for unity. "Teaching is a continual process of searching for wholes and preserving awareness of the inadequacy of any unified conclusion."[23]

Whitehead's rhythmic theory is both confirmed and modified in an interesting way by the empirical research of William Perry on the intellectual and ethical development of college students. Perry discovered that American university students (even at an elite institution, Harvard) are not as far along in intellectual maturation as Whitehead had assumed. They are certainly not at the stage of "generalization" when they enter college. Or rather, the rhythm seems to repeat itself in its own way during the college years, moving from a simple dualism (absolute principles of right and wrong) through various phases of acknowledging diversity and contextual relativism, to the position of recognizing the need for some sort of personal commitment in a relativistic world, which enables one to act on the basis of principles or values. Students move from the "romance" of naive belief, through an incredible deconstruction and disciplining of their minds in a bewildering array of academic perspectives, to the possibility of something like a mature worldview. Perry doubts that many college students actually arrive at the latter, and they may never arrive at it if they do not continue to grow intellectually.[24]

If the rhythm of education arrives at a kind of wisdom that recognizes the necessity of acting on the basis of principles to which one makes an existential commitment, knowing that no construal of reality is ever final and is always relative to interpretive perspectives—knowing that every synthesis of knowledge is only a phase in an ongoing dialectical cycle, knowing that principles are the product of human imagination, insight, and experience—then how is it possible to know anything at all with certainty? This brings us to another important theme of a (post)modern pedagogy—knowledge as constructive and interactive.

CONSTRUCTIVE AND INTERACTIVE KNOWLEDGE

It might appear that the classical theological and philosophical tradition has nothing to say by way of acknowledging the "constructed" character of human knowledge. Ancient Israel believed that the mind of God is revealed in the Torah, and conservative Protestantism has subscribed to a revelational positivism that identifies the very words of scripture with the Word of God. The mainstreams of Jewish and Christian tradition, however, have rejected such literalism. Judaism has known that the Torah requires constant reinterpretation in ever-changing situations, even that its meaning is extended by such interpretation; and the history of such interpretation is the Talmud. While the Torah may be the mirror of the glory of God, it is not that glory itself. It is, in the final analysis, a human mirror and thus a human construction. The glory that shines in the mirror blocks any sensible or verbal representations of God. Thus, paradoxically, we know that we cannot know anything about God except that God is sheer luminosity, a luminosity that illumines, shines within, our own thinking.

The Socratic principle arrives at a similar position. Truth is brought forth by thinking: it is discovered within the subjectivity of the knower, and thus subject and object are ultimately one. In the act of knowing, human beings are connected with reality, and while their intellectual formulations are profoundly shaped by their epistemological categories and their cultural situatedness, they are not delusional fantasies. Through the dialectical method, it is possible to make judgments about truth claims, and these judgments are capable of being tested and verified in a community of discourse. Thus both Socrates and Plato opposed the Sophistic claim that human beings are the measure of all things; rather, that measure is spirit, soul, or God. By virtue of their rationality, human beings participate in this measure but they do not exhaust it.

Awareness of epistemological and cultural relativity has intensified enormously since the Enlightenment. The Enlightenment philosopher Herder was aware that human beings are deeply shaped by history and that everything they know is influenced and limited by their culture, time, and place. But he did not conclude from this that nothing can be known of God. Rather, what is known is that divine providence wants to achieve its aims only through diversity and change; God is revealed precisely in the myriad human constructions of God. This is essentially Hegel's response to the epistemological agnosticism of Kant. Certainly our knowledge of God is a human construction, but God knows and reveals godself through these constructions, even as the rational mystery that is God is never fully grasped by the constructions. In virtue of the fact that we human beings think, we are connected with what is ultimately true and real; we participate in it, but only through a mirror, dimly. We can see God only as reflected in the world and ourselves; otherwise we would be blinded by the divine light. Thought knowing itself implicitly knows God, but Hegel shows that the ways in which thought knows itself are inexhaustible and must not be brought to premature closure; spirit is ever driven beyond itself into the open, the whole, the absolute.

It is important to emphasize that our best intellectual constructions are based on interactions, not on our own isolated subjectivity or opinion. We interact with the processes of knowing itself, with the wealth of traditions, with scholarship and books, with other peoples and cultures, with the natural world and environment, ultimately with the whole that draws us out of ourselves. Knowledge is a social activity, something that occurs in a community of discourse—and this provides a powerful check against its becoming solipsistic, delusional, deceptive, or manipulative. Of course, human beings are tempted by both ambition and anxiety to deceive themselves and others, and often they succeed; but when knowledge is brought into the openness of unfettered communication, such ruses eventually break down. This is why the postmodern emphasis on interactive knowledge and communicative competence is so important. When we are able to test our constructions in the give-and-take of conversation, with the shared objective of achieving a community of free discourse, then we will discover to what extent they are truly a response to something that evokes them and not simply an arbitrary exercise of imagination or a projection of our own subjectivity. In the most poignant moments of teaching and learning, we know that truth is something that gives or manifests itself in the totality of the education-event rather than something we have merely discovered on our own.

Turning now to the recent discussion of pedagogy, one of the most interesting treatments of the constructive or constructed[25] character of knowledge is found in a study of "women's ways of knowing" that was undertaken by Mary Field Belenky and others in response to the work of William Perry.[26] Noting that Perry's study had been based almost entirely on men, the authors sought to duplicate it among women by using a different method. Instead of Perry's sequence of positions moving from dualism to commitment, they identified five roughly parallel epistemological perspectives exemplified by college women: silence, received knowledge, subjective knowledge, procedural knowledge, and constructed knowledge.[27]

The authors named the final perspective "constructed knowledge" (not in opposition to "commitment" but embracing it) because the women they found at this position were intensely self-conscious, aware of their own judgments and desires, concerned about exclusion and inclusion, separation and connection, and wanting their voices and actions to make a

difference in the world. The women had a high tolerance for
contradiction and ambiguity, had abandoned either/or thinking, had learned to live with conflict, and wanted "to embrace
all the pieces of the self in some ultimate sense of the whole,"
avoiding the male tendency to compartmentalize. In brief, these
women had come "to the basic insights of constructivist
thought: *All knowledge is constructed*, and *the knower is an intimate
part of the known.*"[28] Both of these insights deserve emphasis. On
the one hand, to see that all knowledge is a construction and
that truth is context-dependent greatly expands the possibilities
of how to think about anything. It is a great liberation. Theories
are models for approximating experience, and we are not only
free to choose the models and systems we utilize but must also
assume responsibility for them. True experts reveal an appreciation for complexity and a sense of humility about knowledge.
They attend to experience with great care and are not threat-
ened by ambiguity and complexity. They develop the freedom
to move across systems and to make transdisciplinary connections. They know that truth becomes more elusive the older one
grows, and that not the finding but the looking is wonderful.[29]

On the other hand, "when truth is seen as a process of
construction in which the knower participates, a passion for
learning is unleashed. . . . Constructivists become passionate
knowers, knowers who enter into a union with that which is to
be known."[30] Knowing can no longer be abstract and detached
but becomes connected and caring; domination is replaced by
reciprocity and cooperation, readiness to doubt by readiness to
believe, solitary scholarship by a desire for relationships.[31]

The authors pursue the psychological and pragmatic over-
tones of constructivism more clearly than they do the epistemological and ontological ones. When knowers enter into
union with what is to be known through a construction of it,
what actually *is* known? Where and what is truth in this
process? Is it the object under investigation (the *noēma*) or is it
the process of knowing itself (*noēsis*)? Or are these somehow
connected and is the truth in the connection? Is the process of
constructing meaning in an interactive, intersubjective nexus

in some way a mirror, or speculum, of an ultimate relationality that pervades all that is, including God? Is truth to be measured more in its pragmatic effects than in its disclosure of the being of things? These are questions about which postmodernity is genuinely puzzled and divided. We do not have to settle them to acknowledge the impact of viewing knowledge as constructive and interactive.

Bernard Meland provides another helpful approach to the matters we are considering. He notes that the kind of thinking that prevails in much of education today—analytical, descriptive, instrumental—enables students to take things apart, but not to (re)construct or to see things in their relations. By contrast, religious thinking is essentially reflective and constructive thinking—"the kind of thinking that awakens sensibilities, wonder, discernment, appreciation, even reverence where it is proper, in the face of meanings that carry one beyond one's self." Meland believes that creative currents of thought are at work that are reversing the primarily quantitative and functional conception of knowledge associated with the physical and social sciences—currents such as relativity in physics and metaphysics, organism in biology, gestalt in psychology, contextualism and field theory in the social sciences. These tendencies, which are restoring the concern for relations and for integration of knowledge, are religious in that they provide a perspective for thinking in which religious meanings may be discerned. Not only do things exist in relations, but relations are dynamic, and the synthesis of relations can give rise to a qualitative meaning beyond purely functional interests.[32]

Meland identifies several levels of thinking, starting with problem solving, the survey of experience, and critical analysis of experience. A fourth level is "constructive understanding," whose task is that of synthesizing relations such that a larger context of meaning is created. Beyond construction lies "imaginative interpretation," which has an aesthetic quality and elicits insight into fundamental meanings. Finally, in Meland's view, a sixth level combines analysis, constructive understanding, and imaginative interpretation in dealing with large-scale problems of human destiny, namely, theology and metaphysics. It is only at this level that answers can be provided to the question of the relationship between the knower and the known, knowledge and truth, thinking and being.[33]

Certainly there is no consensus in higher education today on these answers; it is enough to hope for openness to the questions and recognition of their importance. We can expect to find a number of partially competing and partially overlapping philosophical construals of the relationship between knowledge and reality—construals as diverse as Hegel's philosophy of spirit, James's radical empiricism, Dewey's pragmatism, Whitehead's philosophy of process, Heidegger's existential ontology, Wittgenstein's view of language, Habermas's theory of communicative action, Derrida's deconstruction of ontotheology. If there is an overlapping among these views, it comes at the point of recognizing the fundamentally interactive and relational character of both knowledge and reality. Mind and world interact; the question is how and to what effect.

At a practical pedagogical level, confirmation of the validity of this insight comes from the success of various forms of interactive teaching. Rather than simply having information presented to them in textbooks and lectures, students are being engaged in the process of identifying assumptions, exploring alternatives, and constructing meaning.[34] Knowledge forms through the interaction between teachers and students, and together they share in the interactivity of the world as a whole. Learning is a connected, cooperative process, and that tells us something about the nature of reality itself. I turn to this matter in the final section of the chapter, but first I want to consider the ethical and pragmatic telos of a postmodern pedagogy, namely, the practice of freedom, which also tells us something about the nature of reality.

EDUCATION AS THE PRACTICE OF FREEDOM

The connection of education and freedom has deep and ancient roots. Education is a kind of liberation from bondage to immediacy, parochialism, and ignorance. By means of education, human selves are gradually opened out to and connected with the world—the world as both a historical process and a natural and social environment. I am not bound to my particular time, place, ethos, family, culture; I am free to travel, to journey in the world of ideas, to make my own way. Education also prepares me to participate as a responsible citizen in the *polis*, the political and social order, so that I have some control over my own destiny as a shared destiny with others. This was certainly Socrates' view of the matter: the telos of education is free citizenship, and the precondition of democracy is an educated citizenry. Socrates established a connection between education and the democratic ideal that is as relevant today as it was two-and-a-half millennia ago. Plato also regarded education as the most fundamental responsibility of the state, but he limited the full benefits of free citizenship to an elite.

These ideas were revisited all too infrequently in the history of Christian theology. Gregory of Nyssa did not consider the political aspect of education, but he did associate it most directly with the process of formation (*morphōsis*) by which human beings become human; and for him Christian paideia was even more than this—it was a renewal, liberation, and *transformation* of human beings through the imitation of Christ. Here for the first time we encounter the language of a transformative pedagogy. This idea was brought into modernity by Herder, who believed that the goal of the educational process is the formation and flourishing of humanity, the realization of freedom and happiness, in ways appropriate to specific times and places. "Human being," he wrote, is "the first liberated being in creation." He associated this liberation with the origin of language, and he regarded education as the means of its fullest actualization.[35]

It was Hegel who definitively associated the themes of education and freedom, *Bildung* and *Freiheit*. The education of each individual is a recapitulation of the cultural development (*Bildung*) of the world, and world history is precisely "the progress of the consciousness of freedom." Freedom is the very substance of human being as conscious of itself and present to itself, and such a being is not a completed entity but is essentially self-producing, engaged in a process of historical becoming. The task of philosophy of history is to comprehend the progression of the consciousness of freedom through the axial turns of world history: the consciousness that *one* is free (the ancient Oriental world), that *some* are free (the Greek and Roman worlds), and that *all* are free (the Christian and European worlds).[36] Education also follows these axial turns: first it is available only to the monarch and his retinue, then to the free male citizens of Greece and Rome, and finally to everybody. The ideal of universal education is implicit in the Christian principle, but it took many centuries to unfold. Hegel was especially insistent about the latter in his *Philosophy of Right*. There, as we have seen, he argued that families and the state have a fundamental responsibility to educate all children, and he was especially concerned about conditions in England where poor children were put to work at an early age in factories and received virtually no education.[37]

Education as viewed by Hegel entails a transition from one kind of freedom, namely, arbitrary, self-seeking free choice, for which he uses the term *Willkür*, to another, which is responsible, intersubjective free will, *freie Wille*. The latter is a communal will, and it requires the creation of social and political institutions that permit freedom to flourish. Hegel envisions a *Reich der Freiheit*, a realm of freedom, which is a secular analogue to the *Reich Gottes*, the realm of God proclaimed by Jesus, and which is also remarkably reminiscent of Aristotle's definition of the *polis* as the *koinōnia tōn eleutherōn*, the community of the free.[38] The community of the free presupposes education.

Hegel would surely have agreed with the Marxist insistence that what is required is not merely the *consciousness* of freedom but the *practice* of freedom. For Hegel there could be no practice without the consciousness, but he did not see as clearly as Marx and his successors that there could be no consciousness without the practice, and that the practice engenders and heightens consciousness, or "conscientizes." Nor did Hegel anticipate that the creation of a truly democratic education would have to challenge some of the cherished assumptions of modern bourgeois capitalist economy. Yet the whole postmodern discussion of conscientization, radical education, critique of dominant discourses, and so forth, is directly traceable to Hegel through Marx and neo-Marxist pedagogies.

Before turning to the latter, we should note that Kierkegaard offers a diametrically opposing strategy. Far from being convinced that it is possible to build a this-worldly realm of freedom with its accompanying educational institutions, Kierkegaard insists on a radical contrast between "Christendom" (the modern bourgeois world) and Christ, who teaches a kind of wisdom that challenges the established economies of the world. Following Christ entails a total change, conversion, rebirth, transformation. For Kierkegaard it does not seem possible that this could become a transformative pedagogy if pedagogy means an institutionalized practice. Rather, what is required is a contemporaneity with Christ that cannot be mediated by any human teacher. Yet something of Kierkegaard's radicalism comes through in the postmodern attacks on "master narratives" and "totalizing systems."

I shall review the recent literature on our present topic under three linked themes: (1) engaged pedagogy and the practice of freedom; (2) radical democracy and social transformation; (3) cultural studies and postcolonial discourses.

1. *Engaged Pedagogy and the Practice of Freedom.* Our first theme is brilliantly articulated by bell hooks.[39] In a passage that could serve as a motto of the present book, she establishes a connection between engaged pedagogy, the practice of freedom, and spiritual formation:

> To educate as the practice of freedom is a way of teaching that anyone can learn. That learning process comes easiest to those of us who teach who also believe that there is an aspect of our vocation that is sacred; who believe that our work is not merely to share information but to share in the intellectual and spiritual growth of our students. To teach in a manner that respects and cares for the souls of our students is essential if we are to provide the necessary conditions where learning can most deeply and intimately begin.[40]

Such teaching requires an engaged pedagogy, that is, one that approaches students with the desire to respond to them as unique beings, that creates relationships based on mutual recognition, and that is also concerned to bring about fundamental changes in the way things are done in the traditional "banking system" of education. In this, bell hooks acknowledges the influence of the Brazilian educator Paulo Freire and the Vietnamese Buddhist monk Thich Nhat Hanh: the teacher is one who both raises consciousness and heals mind and body.

A holistic, engaged pedagogy is even more demanding, bell hooks believes, than a critical or a feminist pedagogy, for it emphasizes well-being, self-actualization, happiness. "If the helper is unhappy, he or she cannot help many people." These very categories are heretical in most higher education. "Indeed, the objectification of the teacher within bourgeois educational structures . . . denigrate[s] notions of wholeness and uphold[s] the idea of a mind/body split, one that promotes and supports compartmentalization." The self is emptied out, leaving only an objective mind, and as a consequence many professors are not interested in spiritual and intellectual guidance but only in the exercise of power and authority. Such teachers cannot practice freedom. If teachers are not themselves engaged in and transformed by the teaching process, they cannot hope to transform their students.[41]

At the heart of engaged pedagogy is a critical thinking practiced in conditions of radical openness and mutuality. Under such conditions, remarks bell hooks, she has been "brought closer . . . to the ecstatic than by most of life's experiences." Somehow discipline and ecstasy come together in practices of freedom, which open up new possibilities and enable students and teachers alike to transgress established boundaries.[42]

One of bell hooks's acknowledged mentors is Paulo Freire, whose work on "conscientization," or "consciousness-raising," has influenced a whole generation of educators.[43] The Portuguese term *conscientização* means both learning to perceive social, political, economic contradictions and taking action against them. By making it possible for human beings "to en-

ter the historical process as responsible subjects," conscientization "enrolls them in the search for self-affirmation and thus
avoids fanaticism." It is rooted in concrete situations of oppression, and its principal method is dialogical, which serves
as the "midwifery" of a "liberating pedagogy," since by means
of it the oppressed bring to conscious awareness the reality of
oppression and find for themselves the themes and resources
for changing it. The objective is not to reverse the oppressor-
oppressed relationship but to overcome it entirely: this is a pedagogy for the "emergence of a new humanity."[44]

Freire's contrast between the "banking model" of education,
in accord with which the teacher simply deposits information in
the student, and the dialogical method of conscientization seems
to be transferable to almost any teaching situation. What Freire
writes here is of great interest. Liberation is not a deposit to be
made in humans; rather, it is a praxis, "the action and reflection
of human beings upon their world in order to transform it."

> Liberating education consists in acts of cognition, not
> transferals of information. It is a learning situation in
> which the cognizable object . . . intermediates the cogni-
> tive actors. . . . The teacher is no longer merely the-one-
> who-teaches, but one who is himself taught in dialogue
> with the students, who in turn while being taught also
> teach. They become jointly responsible for a process in
> which all grow. . . . Authority must be *on the side of* free-
> dom, not *against* it. Here, no one teaches another, nor is
> anyone self-taught. Humans teach each other, mediated
> by the world, by the cognizable objects.[45]

What Freire is saying is that the subject matter teaches itself,
gives itself, and this subject matter is in some ultimate sense always freedom or associated with freedom. Teachers and students are caught up in it. Their dialogical relationship is the
medium in which it appears, but they are not the source of it;
rather, they encounter in their thinking something that transcends both of them. Thus what is to be taught is thinking itself,
not simply specific contents. In the process of thinking, something happens that almost has the quality of "inspiration."

"Education as the practice of freedom . . . denies that human being is abstract, isolated, independent, and unattached to the world; it also denies that the world exists as a reality apart from humans." The truth is that consciousness and the world interact and are co-constitutive. Conscientizing education recognizes not only that consciousness is always changing but also that the world, far from being a static reality, is always in process, in transformation.[46]

2. *Radical Democracy and Social Transformation.* The kind of transformation that Freire and his disciples have in mind is social transformation, and what they envision is a radical form of democracy in which there are no oppressed classes and silenced voices. bell hooks recounts how during the civil rights movement she came to share a "passionate commitment to a vision of social transformation rooted in the fundamental belief in a radically democratic idea of freedom and justice for all." This, she says, is no elaborate postmodern political theory but simply the insight enunciated by Martin Luther King Jr. when he told Americans that we as a nation could not go forward without a "true revolution of values." He warned that "a civilization can flounder as readily in the face of moral and spiritual bankruptcy as it can through financial bankruptcy."[47]

The bankruptcy has become more acute in the thirty years since King uttered these prophetic words. bell hooks wonders what has kept us from moving ahead. Why have we turned away from a commitment to civil rights and social justice to the pursuit of self-interest and the promotion of xenophobia? One primary reason, she says, is that "a culture of domination necessarily promotes addiction to lying and denial."[48] Lies beget more lies until the entire tissue of fabrication comes crashing down. Lies are the deadly enemy of education, which depends on the delicate fabric of truth and trust. Are we to conclude that education for the practice of freedom is failing miserably? At least it helps to remind ourselves that such education has always faced powerful odds and that it requires a commitment for the long term, knowing that the task will never be finished.

Perhaps Henry Giroux is right when he suggests that "radical education" must become more overtly political and pragmatic in its agenda. Schools should educate persons who are able critically to interrogate and resist established social forms rather than to adapt to them—adaptation to the established forms being the agenda of the dominant educational philosophies. Democracy is a celebration of differences, and persons must learn how to play the politics of difference. For this purpose Marxism is no longer the sole or primary resource. There are other critical traditions such as feminist theory, literary criticism, liberation theology, and American populism. Citing Michael Waltzer's ideal of intellectuals as engaged critics, Giroux proposes that teachers should become "transformative intellectuals." They will be engaged but not doctrinaire partisans, bringing their own convictions into a framework that permits debate and is open to critical inquiry. Educators have a public responsibility that involves them in the struggle for democracy. Giroux recognizes what a difficult challenge this is since students and faculty alike today are very complacent and cautious, caught up in market logic and bureaucratic jargon. Critical thinking is submerged in a swamp of red tape, media images, and Web sites.[49]

The task seems more difficult now than it did in the time of John Dewey, who spoke rather easily about the free interplay of ideas and associations in a democratic society. He was certainly right to say that democracy is more than a form of government: "it is primarily a mode of associated living, of conjoint communicated experience."[50] Just this renders it peculiarly vulnerable to distortion by those with the power to control and manipulate communication. Education ought to be the primary medium of communicated experience, but it too has been subverted by the blandishments of image, message, and marketability. Ironically, just as the instruments of communication are expanding exponentially, less and less of substance is communicated. Virtual reality is replacing true reality. We need another Socrates to expose the latest sophistry.

3. *Cultural Studies and Postcolonial Discourses.* Cultural studies, write Henry Giroux and Peter McLaren, "affirm and

demonstrate pedagogical practices engaged in creating a new language, rupturing disciplinary boundaries, decentering authority, and rewriting the institutional and discursive borderlands in which politics becomes a condition for reasserting the relationship between agency, power, and struggle."[51] Commenting on this statement, bell hooks notes that persons engaged in cultural studies must talk to one another, "collaborate in a discussion that crosses boundaries and creates a space for intervention."[52] The primary way of accomplishing this, she believes, is through dialogue across differences—differences in social location, intellectual orientation, race and gender, role and authority. One must put oneself on line, so to speak, and expose one's vulnerabilities. The dialogue does not cause the differences to disappear, but they may become more porous and fluid.

Perhaps all that can be accomplished in some situations is the clarification of differences, and agreement is won only slowly, through conflict and struggle. Indeed, Moacir Gadotti argues that conflict is a necessary ingredient of dialogue, or of what he prefers to call dialectic, especially when conditions of inequality prevail among dialogue partners, as they often do in pedagogical situations. Conflict also arises when educators strive to do more than instill information, Gadotti believes. "Educating presupposes a transformation, and there is no kind of peaceful transformation. There is always conflict and rupture with something, with, for instance, prejudices, habits, types of behaviors, and the like."[53]

As Giroux says, culture is a contested terrain, a site of struggle and transformation.[54] This manifests itself not only in the so-called culture wars but also in postcolonial discourses and border pedagogy. With respect to the culture wars, perhaps the best strategy, as Gerald Graff suggests, is to teach the conflicts themselves, using them to help organize a curriculum and give it focus. He notes that students see the results of conflicts but rarely the discussions and arguments that lead to them. It is important to bring excluded cultures into the curriculum, but unless they are put into dialogue and debate with traditional studies, students will continue to experience a disconnected education.

> Teaching the conflicts has nothing to do with relativism or denying the existence of truth. The best way to make relativists of students is to expose them to an endless series of different positions which are *not* debated before their eyes. Acknowledging that culture is a debate rather than a monologue does not prevent us from energetically fighting for the truth of our own convictions. On the contrary, when truth is disputed, we can seek it only by entering the debate—as Socrates knew when he taught the conflicts two millennia ago.[55]

The conflict of cultures also appears in the form of postcolonialism, which "challenges how imperial centers of power construct themselves through the discourse of master narratives and totalizing systems, . . . relegat[ing] otherness to the margins of power."[56] The rhetoric here is influenced by Michel Foucault, and the assumption is that any culture that attains sufficient power over a long enough period of time will develop colonizing tendencies. The task of postcolonial discourses, then, is to create "a new amalgam of cultural workers" who will, in the words of Cornel West, "historicize, contextualize, and pluralize by highlighting the contingent, provisional, variable, shifting, and changing" in any culture. They will seek to overcome binary oppositions and construct a politics in which differences are honored rather than suppressed or stereotyped.[57] This in turn requires what Giroux calls "border crossings" and a "border pedagogy." As contrasted with multiculturalism, which in his view tends to blur differences and to create depoliticized consensus, the objective should be to create "borderlands" in which diverse cultural resources can fashion new identities. A school should in effect be a cultural borderland, which decenters established authorities even as it refigures disciplinary and pedagogical boundaries.[58]

All this is of course difficult and there are enormous challenges. One is to avoid establishing new canons and colonies that will merely replace the old ones. Another is to assimilate a wealth of new resources without losing the old classics. The practice of freedom demands of us, as Hegel once remarked, hard labor. Freedom is not a goal easily attained, for it requires the interplay of free forces with competing interests and the achievement of productive rather than destructive compromises. The objectives of education are not competition for its own sake but cooperation, not separation but connection. The cooperation and connection can be won only dialectically, not directly. Thus we arrive, also dialectically, at our final theme.

CONNECTED TEACHING AND
COOPERATIVE LEARNING

The themes of connection and cooperation emerged in the classical theological tradition as much in terms of the connection between truth (God) and knowledge (humanity) as in terms of the connection between teachers and students. Indeed, the latter connection was viewed as an analogue of the former. The whole Socratic/Platonic theme of recollection was an instance of this. Human beings are already implicitly connected with the truth, the knowledge of virtue, the eternal ideas. The task of the "midwife" teacher is to elicit this truth from the student through a dialogical process that engenders thinking and overcomes forgetfulness and distortion. The teacher cooperates with the divine paideia just as a midwife cooperates with the birthing process or a physician with the curative powers of nature. Clement of Alexandria made use of the latter analogy, and thus he emphasized that the Word of God uses persuasion and arts of healing rather than force. Christ the Pedagogue leads, guides, steers, navigates. The divine Wisdom is marked by qualities of friendship, benevolence, persuasion, and consolation as well as exhortation, discipline, and censure.

Origen introduced the theme of synergy or cooperation between God's guidance and human action, but it was Gregory of Nyssa who developed it in an original and powerful fashion. As we have seen, it was his view that God cooperates with us rather than we with God. In other words, God finds ways to work in synergy with our own efforts, and so it is with human teachers as well, whose role is to empower students as they actively participate in the educational process. Augustine continued along the same line and went so far as to suggest that, instead of being preoccupied with "what the teacher thinks," students should attend to the subject matters that are conveyed through the teacher. Thomas Aquinas invoked an ancient analogy: just as the physician heals a patient through the activity of nature, so the teacher causes knowledge in a student through the activity of the latter's own natural reason. Humans do not endow the mind with the light of reason but cooperate with it to help it reach the perfection of knowledge.

Calvin was the first to stress the role of the Holy Spirit as inner teacher who penetrates into our hearts and minds. The illumination of the Holy Spirit replaces the Thomistic inner light of reason, but it works in much the same way. The Spirit does not compel or coerce but persuades, draws, inflames; the Spirit "forms our ears to hear and our minds to understand" even more effectively than a human teacher can do. Calvin noted that if words like the promise of salvation do not penetrate into our minds, then they only strike the air and beat upon our ears. This penetration into the mind is the great mystery of education, and for Calvin the Spirit is the "inner schoolmaster" by whom it happens. But human teachers are also needed, for God chooses to teach us by human rather than miraculous and magical means.

Horace Bushnell is of interest here in virtue of his critique of negative pedagogy, which uses force, threats, indoctrination, and punishment as opposed to nurture, which has a mothering quality. The ostrich, he says, is nature's type of all unmotherhood—of teaching by disconnection—since she abandons her young to survive on their own. Human children require close attention, care, guidance, formation, training. Bushnell's use of the metaphor of the mother anticipates the emphasis on connection in "women's ways of knowing."

Indeed, it is the latter work that sets forth the model of "connected teaching" very persuasively. The authors argue that women's experience as mothers provides them with this model as opposed to the banking model or the adversarial model. In place of experts who overwhelm with information, in connected teaching the expert adjusts to the needs and capacities of the learner, just as a mother does for a child, who needs trust and encouragement.[59] Thus women have been attracted to the Socratic model of midwife-teachers, who "do not do students' thinking for them or expect students to think as they do," but who nurture and support them. The first concern of "maternal thinking" and thus also of midwife-teachers is "to preserve the student's fragile newborn thoughts, to see that they are born with their truth intact, that they do not turn into acceptable lies." The second concern is to support the evolution of their students' thinking. They do not say, "You are wrong," but "Think more." They "focus not on their own knowledge (as the lecturer does) but on the students' knowledge." They work through a cycle of confirmation-evocation-confirmation and use their own knowledge to place students in conversation with the larger culture.[60]

The authors provide a rather damaging account of Freire's banking model or, as they describe it, the adversarial model. They do not say that this is a "male" model as opposed to a "female" model, but they seem to think that male professors are especially prone to it. Students take the teacher's words as sacrosanct and deposit them in their notebooks. The teacher takes few risks: he composes his thoughts in silence and, while students are permitted to see the product of his thinking, the process of gestation is hidden from view. He invites students to find holes in his argument, but he has taken pains to make it airtight. He is proud of the rigor of his interpretation, and the students admire it too, but there is no sharing in the thinking process. The authors claim that this problem is especially acute in science, which is often regarded as "the quintessentially masculine intellectual activity." Here professors tend to present interpretive models as though they are simple facts, leaving students with the impression that "science is not a creation of the human mind." As Perry says, teachers first appear in the guise of gods and are later revealed to be human. This model is wrong for women, conclude the authors. Surely they do not think it is right for men.[61]

Assuming the desirability of connected teaching, what is the appropriate connection between teachers and students? Belenky and her colleagues believe that the connections should be viewed as temporary affiliations, or short-term partnerships, as opposed to long-term personal relationships. Aside from the risks of the latter, including the potential for abuse or confusion of roles, a teacher simply cannot establish a time-consuming personal relationship with many students and needs rather to be "totally and nonselectively present" to each and every student at specific times. In the teacher-student relationship, the personal must become the professional, and the professional personal. "A connected teacher is not just another student; the role carries special responsibilities. It does not entail power over the students; however, it does carry authority, an authority based not on subordination but on cooperation."[62]

Martin Buber touches on this question in an illuminating way. Education, he believes, is a basic form of dialogical relationship, a communion that entails neither will to power nor eros but a kind of asceticism, or reserve. Teachers exercise responsibility for a group of lives entrusted to them for their influence but not their interference. The elemental experience of the teacher is that of "experiencing the other side." This is more than empathy; it is inclusion, recognition of the other's legitimacy, of his or her stance before the eternal Other. The teacher becomes a medium through which a selection of the world affects this other person. "What is otherwise found only as grace, inlaid in the folds of life—the influencing of the lives of others with one's own life—becomes here a function and a law. . . . Without the action of his spirit being in any way weakened [the teacher] must at the same time be over there, on the surface of that other spirit which is being acted upon." But the relationship of inclusion cannot be mutual in the case of education. The teacher "experiences the pupil's being educated, but the pupil cannot experience the educating of the educator. The educator stands at both ends of the common situation, the pupil only at one end. In the moment when the pupil is able to throw himself across and experience from over there, the educative relation would be burst asunder, or change into friendship." Friendship is based on "a concrete and mutual experience of inclusion." It is "the true inclusion of one another by human souls."[63]

Is friendship really excluded from the educative relationship? Perhaps there are instances of proto-friendship with older and more mature students, students who are in process of becoming colleagues in the project of education, but on the whole I think Buber's caution, his insistence on an ascetic quality to the relationship, is well advised. This does not mean that teachers and students cannot be friendly, cannot have fun with each other, cannot interact and engage each other, cannot love each other with an inclusive love, cannot enjoy each others' embodied presence.[64] But all of this should occur under a kind of constraint that recognizes the distinctive character of the relationship and does not violate it.[65]

Cooperative learning occurs in response to, or as an expression of, the connection between teachers and students. As Gabriel Moran points out, there is no actual teaching without learning, just as in baseball there is no actual hit until the bat connects with the ball (and, as we know, most swings are misses). Teaching-learning is a mysterious continuum that cannot be described in terms of cause and effect. There is a single actualization of teaching-learning that can be viewed from opposite ends but that occurs only in the student. Ironically, the teacher's effort does not bring about the student's learning, and often what the student learns does not correspond to the teacher's intent. The greatest teachers know that only occasionally are they truly teachers. The best they can do is to design a productive environment in which teaching-learning might occur, or to show by their own example how to live, think, act, and die. This indirect "showing how" is the essential pedagogical act: Moran refers to it as a "mystical" strand in education that has been appreciated by sources as diverse as Ludwig Wittgenstein and Thomas Aquinas, and within Eastern religions.[66]

In this sense, all of learning is cooperative, or as we have said earlier, interactive. In a more specific sense, cooperative learning refers to a pedagogical strategy in which small groups of students work together toward a common goal. Here students are cooperating with one another rather than competing or working individually, and studies indicate that it is a superior method of learning. Cooperative, or active, learning components can be built into a class session in a great variety of ways, interwoven with lectures and other forms of presentation. Cooperation occurs not only among students but also between teachers and students; and (as Gregory of Nyssa long ago recognized) it appears to be most effective when teachers cooperate with students rather than students with teachers. The role of the teacher "shifts from expert/authority figure to facilitator/coach, one who unobtrusively circulates, observes, monitors, and answers questions."[67] Here the initiative in the educational relationship moves to students. Perhaps it would be better to say that the initiative shifts back and forth in accord with the rhythmic process of education. There is no single center and norm but a fluid encompassing process.

Another instance of cooperative learning takes the form of curricular integration, when teachers and students from different specialized disciplines come together to create a learning community out of their differences. Gerald Graff says that these are best elicited from already existing practices rather than being imposed by an overarching plan; they can take the form of jointly taught courses, teacher swapping, courses clustered around a common theme or central controversies, symposia on interdisciplinary topics, and writing across the curriculum.[68] The possibilities for cooperation in an educational process are almost endless when people begin to think about them and are willing to make the effort to accomplish them.

In this chapter I have identified several elements of a transformative pedagogy, drawing on a wealth of modern and postmodern resources while reminding myself that these themes also are anticipated in the classical tradition. It is clear that education is a crucial element in the formation of human lives. But what renders it not merely formative but transformative? Transformation suggests a change from one condition to another, and it implies a process with a goal, a vision of something to be accomplished.

What are the change, process, and vision? The change seems to be from a condition of ignorance, illusion, forgetfulness, closure, isolation, and alienation to one of knowledge, truth, recollection, openness, connection, and reconciliation. The process is a rhythmic one, moving through cycles of engagement, discipline, and generalization by which wisdom is gradually acquired about truth and illusion, good and evil, in a complex and tragically conflicted world. The vision is one of human flourishing, both of individuals and the body politic; and flourishing seems to have to do with the fullest possible actualization of freedom for each and every person and for the people as a whole, the *dēmos*. Human beings are intrinsically free beings, and education is their liberation, their coming into their own as humans. But how is all of this possible? We are talking about something like a fall, redemption, conversion, consummation, and that not only is religious language but points to a spiritual process.[69] Can the "foolishness" of human wisdom accomplish this radical sort of transformation? Or is it the work of "God's Wisdom"—not acting alone of course, but as the energizing, drawing, driving paideutic force?

4

God's Wisdom

Education as Paideia

Just as human beings are not the measure of all things, so also human wisdom is not the redemption of all things, the power by which everything is transformed. How, then, is a transformative pedagogy possible? My attempt to answer this question draws the resources from the previous two chapters together into a constructive endeavor, a theology of education whose guiding premise is that for education to happen in its fullest and most radical sense the paideutic power of God is required. This is what makes education an intrinsically religious endeavor.

In his First Letter to the Corinthians, the Apostle Paul has some things to say about wisdom (*sophia*) (1 Cor. 1:18–31). He quotes the Prophet Isaiah: "I [the Lord] will destroy the wisdom of the wise, and the discernment of the discerning I will thwart" (Isa. 29:14 Greek). For Paul this means that God has "made foolish the wisdom of the world," or, more precisely, that "the world did not know God through wisdom" (1 Cor. 1:20–21). Paul assumes that this weakness of human wisdom must be part of the divine plan or purpose so that God can bring about salvation through "Christ crucified"—who is "a stumbling block to Jews and foolishness to Gentiles" (1:23). We can, I think, prescind from Paul's judgment about God's plan while agreeing with his observation that human wisdom for the most part is not only "boastful" (1:31) but weak and foolish. This can be read in one of two ways: the more radical, Kierkegaardian reading that views human wisdom as utterly corrupt, empty, sinful, so that the Socratic project of recollection is doomed to failure;

or the more moderate, Catholic reading that considers some sort of synergy or cooperation to be necessary between the inner divine light of reason (or the inner illumination of the Holy Spirit for the Reformed tradition) and human cognitive powers, which are prone to self-deception or illusion and limited by the finitude and sinfulness of human experience. Both readings can appeal to Paul. Although I believe Kierkegaard's reading is closer to Paul's paradoxical formulations in this text, I propose to follow the more moderate reading.

What is of particular interest to me is Paul's association of "the power of God and the Wisdom of God" with Jesus Christ (1:24, 31). Paul emphasizes "Christ crucified," but I shall emphasize "Christ incarnate" (an important aspect of which is the way Christ died). Thus Jesus of Nazareth is the incarnation of God's Wisdom; as such, he is the prophet and teacher of Wisdom, and the wisdom he teaches has redemptive, transformative power in the world. "God's Wisdom, secret and hidden" (2:7) must become incarnate, must assume human form if it is to in-form and trans-form human wisdom. Thereby a christological element is introduced into our discussion that thus far has been lacking. I do not mean to claim that God's Wisdom is incarnate *only* in the figure of Jesus of Nazareth. The latter figure is rather a model, or paradigm, for understanding how God's Wisdom becomes incarnate in many forms of human wisdom and a multitude of educational endeavors as the energizing, drawing, driving paideutic force. There is a pedagogy of the divine Wisdom that can be named "paideia."

Such is the argument of this chapter, which starts by inquiring into the meaning of "wisdom" as a trope of God's pedagogical presence in the world, then moves on to a consideration of the "incarnation" of divine Wisdom in Jesus Christ, and concludes by examining the distinctive pedagogy of God's Wisdom.

THE FIGURE OF WISDOM:
SOPHIA/SPIRIT

Our words "wise" and "wisdom" derive from an Indo-European root, *weid-*, meaning "to see" or "to know." They are related to the Sanskrit *vēdas*, "knowledge"; to the Greek *eidos*, "idea," "form," "seeing"; to the Latin *videre*, "to see"; to the old German *wissago*, a "seer" or "prophet"; and to the modern German *wissen*, "to know." Expanding on these etymological hints metaphorically, we can say that "wisdom" means an insightful seeing or visioning, an intellectual intuiting or imagining, through which something takes form (mental and/or visual) and a practice ensues. The connection of wisdom with both vision (insight into what is hidden, mysterious) and practice (practical knowledge, *phronēsis*) is ancient and well established.[1]

Recent discussions of theological knowledge and education have appropriated the term "wisdom" in this broad sense. Edward Farley says that wisdom is a new posture of the heart that comes with redemption; it is founded in God and is directed toward other human beings, the self, nature, and the world. It is a turning toward reality rather than a turning away from it; it is oriented to truth rather than illusion. Theology in the classical sense is not a technical discipline for scholars but "the wisdom proper to the life of the believer." As wisdom, theology is a kind of meta-thinking or paideia about a "mystery which resists partitioning" into scientific specializations.[2] Similarly, John Cobb writes that "wisdom is a way of seeing things in the complexity of their ever-changing relationships. . . . Wisdom is qualitative; it makes judgments of importance and desirability." Information, by contrast, is quantitative and is produced by technology and specialization. Cobb's concern is that universities as a whole and theological schools in particular have been turned into information factories that require the disciplinary organization of knowledge but have lost sight of wisdom.[3] David Kelsey agrees with Farley that, for the theological tradition at least through the Reformation, "to understand God is to have a kind of wisdom or *sapientia*. . . . This wisdom concerning God embraces contemplation, discursive reasoning, the affections, and the actions that comprise a Christian's life." Kelsey notes that the elements included in wisdom can be construed quite differently depending on how they are related and which is made central. He is not sanguine that they can be properly integrated in our own time, and he discerns an abiding tension between wisdom as paideia and specialized scientific knowledge.[4] This is a matter to which I shall return later in this chapter and in the final chapter.

The knowledge of God is a kind of wisdom. Is the God who is thus known also a kind of Wisdom? Is there a divine Wisdom that engenders human wisdom? So it seems for the Jewish Wisdom traditions. Originally God was depicted as providing the definitive *teaching* through the Torah, which reveals the very mind of God, but not as the active *teacher* who interacts with learners, providing insight and inspiration, leading them out of themselves into the divine mystery. In later Judaism, however, three primary mediators, figures, or personifications of the divine power and presence in the world began to appear: Wisdom, Word, and Spirit. Already in ancient times theologians such as Saint Jerome noted that Wisdom is consistently feminine in grammatical gender across Hebrew (*hokhmah*), Greek (*sophia*), and Latin (*sapientia*), while Word is consistently masculine (*dabar, logos, verbum*) and Spirit is mixed, being feminine in Hebrew (*ruach*), neuter in Greek (*pneuma*), and masculine in Latin (*spiritus*).

Feminist theologians have seized on this fact and have argued that of these three figures Wisdom is the most developed representation in the Hebrew scriptures of God's presence and activity: Wisdom appears in Job, Proverbs, the Wisdom of Solomon, Sirach (Ecclesiasticus, or the Wisdom of Jesus Son of Sirach), and Baruch. In later Judaism and early Christianity, precisely because of her feminine identity, Wisdom (Sophia) was largely displaced by Word (Logos) and Spirit. But in the Wisdom literature, writes Elizabeth Johnson, Wisdom is consistently female, "casting herself as sister, mother, female beloved, chef and hostess, preacher, judge, liberator, establisher of justice, and a myriad of other female roles wherein she symbolizes transcendent power orienting and delighting the world. She pervades the world, both nature and human beings, interacting with them all to lure them along the right path to life."[5] Thus it is appropriate to refer to Wisdom by her Greek name, Sophia. "Sophia is Israel's God in female imagery," an imagery that stresses God's nearness, activity, and summons.[6] Elisabeth Schüssler Fiorenza notes that the female figure of Wisdom is traceable not only to the feminine gender of the word in Hebrew and Greek but also to sociological changes. After the exile and loss of the monarchy, Israel shifted to a family-centered society in which women had a more prominent role and were often idealized. The figure of Wisdom may have been patterned on actual women, and an ascetic Wisdom community of women and men may have existed. Woman Wisdom is called sister, spouse, mother, beloved, teacher. She searches the streets for people, invites them to her table, offers life, knowledge, rest, salvation for all who will accept her. Initially she resides in Israel, her very special people, but the later apocalyptic Wisdom theology suggests that she has not found a place and has returned to heaven, where she dwells with God and is the glory of God, a collaborator in God's work, a pure effervescence of the divine light.[7]

I am especially interested in the communicative, revelatory, pedagogical work of Wisdom in this literature, for it is this work that is most closely associated with her name as the one who gives vision, insight, and knowledge; she gives it because she *is* the divine light, the divine revelation, the divine teaching *and* the divine teacher. Wisdom appears as a prophet of God in Proverbs 1–9, crying out her message in the streets and at the town gates. In the book of Sirach, she proclaims that she has come forth from God, is born from God's mouth as a Word of God (Sir. 24:3–7). Sirach goes further and identifies Wisdom with the Torah (Sir. 24:22–23; cf. Bar. 3:9–4:4), thus establishing a specific link between the divine teaching and the divine teacher. "Draw near to me, you who are uneducated, and lodge in the house of instruction" (Sir. 51:23). In the Wisdom of Solomon there is a great celebration of divine Wisdom, who is readily accessible to those who seek her and is the source of all knowledge:[8]

There is in her a spirit that is intelligent, holy,
unique, manifold, subtle,
mobile, clear, unpolluted,
distinct, invulnerable, loving the good, keen,
irresistible, beneficent, humane,
steadfast, sure, free from anxiety,
all-powerful, overseeing all,
and penetrating through all spirits
that are intelligent, pure, and altogether subtle.

For wisdom is more mobile than any motion;
because of her pureness she pervades and penetrates all things.

For she is a breath of the power of God,
and a pure emanation of the glory of the Almighty;
therefore nothing defiled gains entrance into her.

For she is a reflection of eternal light,
a spotless mirror of the working of God,
and an image of his goodness.

Although she is but one, she can do all things,
and while remaining in herself, she renews all things;
in every generation she passes into holy souls
and makes them friends of God, and prophets;
for God loves nothing so much as the person who lives with
     wisdom.

(Wisd. 7:22–28)

The purity, mobility, and subtleness of Wisdom, or Sophia, her ability to penetrate all things, to penetrate through intelligent spirits, to pass into holy souls and make them friends of God, indicate her essentially spiritual, communicative, intelligible quality. She works inwardly, infusing herself into human minds and hearts, renewing and moving them toward what is good, beneficent, humane. She is oriented to practices, not simply knowledge for the sake of knowledge; her seeing-showing is a "seeing how" and a "showing how." Despite her manifold presence, she remains one, within herself, for she is a reflection of eternal light, a speculum of the glory of God. She is Spirit, "a breath (*ruach*) of the power of God," of the same substance as human spirits and thus able to communicate with them. This is a fluid, moving, mobile substance that is purely relational in quality; it moves, connects and disconnects rhythmically, as thinking does, or as subatomic quanta of energy. Wisdom is not a quantity that is depleted: she remains within herself even as she passes into other spirits.

Both Sophia and Spirit are, in Johnson's words, "symbols of God's energy involved in universal cosmic quickening, inspiring the prophetic word of justice, renewing the earth and the human heart." They are represented by common symbols such as a bird or dove, and they are both manifestations of the *shekinah*, the dwelling or presence of the divine glory.[9] They are closely identified with each other in the book of Wisdom, and, as we shall see, they come together again in Jesus of Nazareth. In early Christianity, the masculine persona Logos tended to displace the feminine figure Sophia, and Irenaeus, for example, determined that Word and Spirit are the two "hands" by which God the Father acts in the world as revealer, creator, redeemer. But it is noteworthy that Irenaeus also identified the Spirit with the divine Wisdom, following Theophilus rather than Justin Martyr in this regard.[10] Here Wisdom seems to be the more encompassing figure or persona, including both God's rationality (Logos) and God's spirituality (Spirit). God's Spirit is rational, logical Spirit and thus Wisdom.

From another point of view, Spirit is the more encompassing figure of the divine presence, while Sophia is a more determinate figure, a concrete manifestation, or modality, of God's Spirit. Sophia defines the kind of Spirit that God's Spirit is—not a possessing, displacing, controlling Spirit, but a persuading, inviting, educing, communicating, teaching Spirit, acting in profound interaction with human spirit, indeed the whole cosmos. God's indwelling Spirit has the quality of wisdom rather than of raw force, of education rather than compulsion. In an earlier work I have attempted to develop a theology of the Spirit oriented to the motifs of energy, relationality, rationality, communication, and emergence.[11] Here I am focusing on Wisdom as God's educative Spirit, that is, as a figure or persona of

God's pedagogical presence in the world. But regardless where the stress is placed, these two figures are essentially the same, each defining the other, hence the slash, "Sophia/Spirit."

By using the terms "figure" and "persona," I am attempting to avoid the suggestion that Sophia/Spirit is a divine person in the sense of a distinct center of consciousness interacting with two other divine persons, the Father and the Son, to form a Trinity of three persons. The *one God* is personal, not *a* person but *the* person—personhood or "personeity"—in a sense that we can only faintly imagine from our own experience of being persons. This one divine person subsists in various modes of relationality that have been named by the tradition "Father" (more satisfactorily, "Father/Mother"), "Son" (or "Christ," "Logos"), and "Spirit" (or "Wisdom"). These are not persons in the sense of independent self-consciousnesses but rather *personae,* roles or functions performed in a social context that come to be identified with specific configurations of action. We might say that the personae are "personifications" or "imperson-ations" of God in the world in the sense that God becomes configured or incarnate in distinctive forms of personal, inter-personal, and transpersonal activity—the figure of the Fa-ther/Mother in the creation of persons (as well as of other beings), the figure of the Son/Christ in the person of Jesus of Nazareth, the figure of Sophia/Spirit in individual believers and the community of faith.[12] The earliest christology links the second and third personifications: God's Wisdom becomes in-carnate in a special way in Jesus of Nazareth, making him the Christ, the messianic prophet and teacher.

THE INCARNATION OF WISDOM
Jesus as Prophet and Teacher of Wisdom[13]

In Philippians 2:5–11, Paul adopts an older christological hymn, which says that the "form of God . . . emptied itself" and took on the "form of . . . a human being." This human form, or figure, which was that of a servant, entailed humility and obe-dience to the point of death but also exaltation and honor. In the version of the hymn that Paul gives, the subject of this activity (the one who was "in" the form of God), was "Christ Jesus"—language that suggests a preexistent divine Son or Logos. But the christological language may well have been grafted onto what was originally a hymn to Wisdom, so that the original reference of the "who" in verse 6, a reference that is grammatically awkward, was not to Christ but to the Wisdom of God—this Wisdom being the form or persona of God that took on human form.[14]

A number of recent scholars, among them Elisabeth Schüssler Fiorenza, have argued that the Jesus movement may have been part of a first-century Jewish Wisdom community in which women as well as men played a prominent role. It was an emancipatory movement, hoping for the liberation of Israel from political and cultural domination. This liberation was to be accomplished not by revolutionary struggle but with the coming of a messianic prophet and teacher in whom Wisdom fully dwelt and by whom the *basileia tou theou,* the kingdom or domain of God, would be inaugurated. Jesus emerged as a leader in this community, and a number of people came to believe that he was the promised prophet-teacher.[15] Schüssler Fiorenza says that two levels of reflection are discernible in the earliest Christian Wisdom discourses. "The first level, which may go back to the historical Jesus himself but is barely traceable any longer, understands Jesus as messenger and prophet of Sophia. The second level of theological reflection identifies Jesus with Divine Wisdom. Jesus, however, is not called 'Sophia' but receives 'male' christological titles such as *kyrios* and *sōtēr.*" Between these two levels there may have been "a transitional stage in which attributes of Sophia were given to Jesus."[16] The first level is found in the Sayings Source (Q) believed to lie behind portions of the Gospels of Matthew and Luke; the transitional phase appears in certain pre-Markan and pre-Pauline traditions (such as the christological hymn in Philippians); and the second level is identified with the theologies of Paul, Matthew, and John.

References to Wisdom/Sophia are found explicitly in a few passages of the Sayings Source, and they are implicit in others.[17] Against attempts to divide the followers of Jesus and John the

Baptist, Jesus claims that "Wisdom is vindicated by *all* her children" (Luke 7:35). Wisdom is the one who sends "prophets and
apostles, some of whom they [this generation] will kill and per-
secute" (Luke 11:49). In lamenting on Jerusalem, "the city that
kills the prophets and stones those who are sent to it," Jesus remarks, "How often have I desired to gather your children together as a hen gathers her brood under her wings, and you were
not willing! . . . I tell you, you will not see me until the time comes
when you say, 'Blessed is the one who comes in the name of the
Lord'" (Luke 13:34–35). From these fragments (together with
corroborating evidence from other Wisdom sources), we may
conclude that Sophia has many children, among whom are num-
bered the prophets and apostles, and Sophia's children are likely
to suffer abuse and rejection at the hands of the world. Her children are presently scattered about, but she will gather them and
be vindicated by them. She will outlast the powerful and out-
smart the wise, and her children will be empowered to continue
the struggle on behalf of God's project or inheritance (*basileia*).
Jesus is preeminent among these children because he taught in
the Wisdom tradition of parables, proclaiming thereby the in-
breaking of God's project, and he engaged in a praxis of inclusive wholeness, gathering all who would follow him. Sophia
dwells in him fully but also transcends him, drawing him into
contact with others, to whom he ministers and from whom he
draws strength—women, tax collectors and sinners, Samaritans
and Syro-Phoenicians, the sick and poor, children and old folk,
ultimately the whole of humanity. Jesus' followers will carry on
Sophia's mission and message despite—indeed because of—his
death, which is not an end but a beginning ("he is not here [in
the tomb], . . . but is going ahead of you to Galilee" [Mark
16:6–7]). His message, or cause, is the important thing, and Wisdom lives on in the continuing cause.

Jesus' cause is that of the kingdom, project, or inheritance of
God, the *basileia tou theou*. Is there a connection between the
source and the substance of Jesus' proclamation, that is, between
these two intriguing images (both feminine in gender), *sophia*
and *basileia*? I believe there is. Wisdom names the constitutive

power of the basileia—a rationality, discourse, or logic that is radically communicative, aimed at the overthrow and reshaping of all established structures and authorities. This is an eminently practical wisdom, issuing in communities of solidarity and mutuality. It engenders the practice of its own substance, which is freedom. In this sense, the basileia is a pedagogical project: it is paideia in the practice of freedom. The Wisdom of God is the new logic, the logic of grace and freedom by which the basileia overturns the oppressive logic of the world, and it is the spiritual power that shapes Jesus into becoming the proclaimer and bearer of the basileia. The logic and power of divine Wisdom are, in a single expression, "communicative freedom." Understood in this way, Wisdom encompasses yet transcends both Logos and Spirit. Jesus is the Word of God and the Spirit of God because he is the Wisdom of God, the incarnation of God's caring, truthful, communicative Sophia, who sets us free from the lying, foolishness, and boasting of this world.

In the preceding paragraph I have begun to make the transition from understanding Jesus as the definitive (though not exclusive) prophet and teacher of Wisdom to understanding him as the bearer of Wisdom, the one in whom Wisdom is incarnate. This transition is inevitable since the latter is implicit in the former: Jesus is *the* prophet and teacher *because* Wisdom is incarnate in him. This is the transition that the New Testament traditions themselves make as their movement is traced through the pre-synoptic and pre-Pauline strata to the writings of Paul and the Gospels. It would take us too afar afield to survey this rich material. Rather, I shall focus on one question: What does it mean to say that Wisdom becomes "incarnate" (en-fleshed, embodied) in a human being—or, in the words of the pre-Pauline christological hymn, that the form of God "empties itself" and "takes on" the form of a human being? How does such a thing come about? The New Testament literature itself offers remarkably little speculation about this question, perhaps because the earlier traditions at least assume the simplest and most obvious answer: that the Spirit of God, appearing in the persona of Wisdom, indwelt and in-spirited the human spirit of Jesus. If God is Spirit, and if human beings are spirits, then surely such a thing is possible. The assumption of the entire Hebraic tradition is that God's *shekinah*, the presence of the divine glory, is able to dwell in the midst of and within God's people. The glory appears in countless human forms and faces. This is a presence of Spirit to spirit that empowers and enlivens but does not displace the human spirit. The incarnation, or in-forming, of God's Spirit in human spirits is by no means restricted to one human being, Jesus of Nazareth, but for the followers of Jesus the coming to speech of God's Wisdom in him is powerfully disclosive of God's reality and purpose. This understanding of incarnation is far removed from the quasi-physical theories of later Christian orthodoxy according to which Jesus Christ is literally a god in human flesh.

What is distinctive about Jesus is not incarnation as such but the uniquely powerful manifestation of divine Wisdom in his teaching, which is at one with his praxis of care, healing, and gathering. His teaching assumes a normative, paradigmatic quality in human history. It simply has had the power in a profound way to draw people out of their daily preoccupations and petty provincialisms into an encounter with the eternal, with ultimate truth and value, with unbounded love, with a radical, transformative freedom. Jesus does not set this forth in a series of propositions, laws, or theoretical statements. Rather, very much like Socrates, he engages in conversation with people, forcing them to reflect on their own traditions and to think about their deeper meaning. Rather than offering something totally new, Jesus radicalizes the shared traditions. He is the teacher who brings the teaching of the Torah alive in such a remarkably direct and powerful way that its implications for daily life could not be avoided. In this he is a new Moses who dares to challenge the authority of Moses for the sake of Moses and his people. He teaches with an authority that is evident to all who hear him (Matt. 7:29). He is called "Rabbi" or "Teacher" (John 1:38, cf. Matt. 23:7), a salutation that links him more closely with Judaism than any other (christological) title.

Jesus does something that Socrates did not do, namely, he

tells stories, or parables—parables that symbolically evoke and enact God's basileia, God's "freedom project," in which the logic of domination, violence, reward, and punishment that prevails in the everyday world is challenged and replaced by a new logic, the logic of grace, compassion, and freedom, which points to a new kind of communal existence in which each person exists for the sake of the other, a community of mutuality and inclusive wholeness. This is how and what Jesus teaches, and it marks him as the one in whom God's very own Wisdom comes to speech, encountering and reorienting human wisdom, deflating its boastfulness, mending its foolishness, empowering its weakness. Like Socrates, the truth of what he teaches is inscribed on his own body in the form of suffering and execution at the hands of those who find the teaching deeply threatening.

Jesus' teaching continues to work salvifically or redemptively. There is nothing magical about it. By virtue not so much of its content as its way of thinking and being, it provides resources by which, again and again, human beings can break the grip of the dominant paradigms, battle against illusion and fear, find purpose in life, and participate in the open-ended, never-finished project of building a new world. This teaching is unbreakably linked with the teacher, the one who enacted in his own life, ministry, suffering, and death the truth of the teaching. In this instance, the teaching would be nothing without the teacher, and the teacher without the teaching. Kierkegaard is partly right in this respect about the difference between Socrates and Christ. Here the teaching and the teacher are one and the same; they blend into each other in such a way that we understand the meaning of the teaching through the example of the teacher (he "shows us how"[18]), and we understand the identity of the teacher through the redemptive quality of his teaching (it reveals him to be *God's* Wisdom). The person and work of Christ are inseparable.

It is noteworthy that the earliest post-biblical christologies were Spirit or inspiration christologies and thus closely connected with the Wisdom tradition. The adoptionism of Paul of

Samosata attributed to Christ the status of a human being pre-
eminently endowed; the relation of the Word to Jesus was a
kind of indwelling, participation, grace, or quality (*poiotēs*). For
the Apostolic Fathers of the second century (Ignatius, Bar-
nabas, Hermas), the divine element in Christ was the preexistent Spirit. Apologists such as Justin Martyr, influenced by
Stoicism, regarded the germinal Logos (*logos spermatikos*) to in-
dwell Jesus like a seed; and Irenaeus understood the Logos to
be the "form" or "shape" (*morphē*) in which the godhead manifests itself. For the Dynamic Monarchianists and Modalists of
the third century, Jesus was a human being upon whom God's
Spirit or Wisdom descended at birth, baptism, or transfigura-
tion. This trajectory came to early fruition in the Antiochene
christology of the fourth century, after which it was suppressed
by orthodox Chalcedonianism, which posited a physical union
of the person of the divine Logos with human flesh. Against
this Theodore of Mopsuestia insisted that the Logos indwelt a
complete, active human being. Godhead is present everywhere
in terms of being and activity, whereas the union in Christ is by
favor or grace. Nestorius considered that each of the natures in
Christ, the divine and human, has its own *prosōpon,* or persona,
but they become one persona in the Incarnate. This is not a
union (*henōsis*) but a perfect and continuous conjunction
(*synapheia*); the Word indwelt Jesus by grace (*kat' eudokian*).[19]

In recent years this ancient christological pattern has been
newly appreciated. The inspiration christology of Geoffrey
Lampe and John Hick is one example;[20] the Wisdom christology
of Denis Edwards is another.[21] I wish to call attention to the work
of Douglas Ottati, who is not, I think, attempting to retrieve Wisdom motifs, but rather attempting to make a contemporary
statement within the Reformed tradition.[22] He identifies the
"distinctive pattern" of Christ's work as follows: he *teaches the
truth* about God and human life, he *embodies a way* of living that
coheres with the truth, and he *empowers life* by his sacrifice and
example. What the Reformed tradition called the prophetic, the
kingly, and the priestly work of Christ can be described as the
pedagogical, ethical, and saving aspects of his work; together

they comprise his "engendering deed." The first, Christ's prophetic activity, refers to the portrayal of Jesus in the Gospels as one who teaches with authority and is called "Rabbi" or "Teacher."[23] Jesus teaches not in a narrow doctrinal sense; rather, he teaches "the truth about history" as God's governance and the truth about the world as the realm of God's grace. He teaches the value of love, humility, care, nonviolence, trust, loyalty, self-denial. By his teaching and deed, he imparts the saving power of God, the power of conversion and transformation, the power of the cross to turn and to renew life. The threefold work reflects Jesus' distinct identity (his "person") as the supreme mediator of the reality of God. He is a "God-shaped" human being, radically oriented to God through the real presence of the Spirit of God in him. Jesus Christ is the *charaktēr* or *eikōn* of God in whom is revealed "the fullness of God's dynamic relationality to all things." As such, he is a "pattern or symbolic form" that "informs our vision of God." These formulations nicely summarize the christological approach I am attempting to establish.

Another distinct advantage to understanding Jesus Christ as Teacher is the congeniality of this model with African and Asian cultures. Recent attempts at christological construction drawing on indigenous African traditions have portrayed Christ as the "wise ancestor" who places his descendants in contact with the source of life, or as the teacher and master of initiation, the elder of the community who initiates the people into the way of life.[24] The figure of the teacher, sage, or guru is especially prominent in Asian religions. Both Christ and Buddha—Jesus of Nazareth and Siddhartha Gotama—may be viewed as teachers of enlightenment and mediators of liberation who focused on the ultimate concerns of human beings in concrete situations. They taught a saving, practical knowledge rather than theoretical truths, and they exemplified their teachings by their actions. Another obvious point of contact is between understanding Christ as the "way" to truth and life and the "way of change" in Taoism.[25]

The most interesting recent attempt at constructing a cross-cultural christology is found in the work of M. Thomas

Thangaraj, who focuses on the Hindu concept of "guru" as used by Tamil Saivites in South India.[26] To understand Christ as "guru" clearly stands in the trajectory of interpretations that have viewed Jesus as a teacher or rabbi, one filled by the Wisdom of God. This, Thangaraj claims, is a much more promising approach than that of regarding Jesus as an *avatar*, a more or less physical incarnation of a deity. Gurus exist only in *relation* to disciples; it is the recognition and affirmation of the latter that constitutes a guru's guruship. The guru *functions* as God to the disciples; he makes God's presence real to them. This points toward a functional, relational, and public christology as opposed to a metaphysical, substantial, and private one. Above all, Jesus the guru *teaches*, and the way that he teaches both fulfills and modifies the guru-concept of the Saivites: his is a public, non-elitist teaching; he teaches with an authority attributable solely to his unique relationship with God and his unreserved identification with his hearers; he teaches by way of persuasion and invitation rather than demand; and his is a praxis-oriented pedagogy. The central symbol of his teaching, the *basileia tou theou*, provides a vision of God, of human community, and of the problem of the human condition—the three themes addressed by every guru. In virtue of his death and resurrection, he himself becomes the way, the truth, and the life of which he spoke: the teacher-guru becomes the crucified guru. In sum, Thangaraj's work demonstrates the tremendous potential for comparative and cross-cultural theology opened up by an understanding of Jesus as the prophet and teacher of Wisdom.

Pedagogical Models of Redemption

The same potential in a Wisdom approach applies as we shift our attention from the person to the work of Christ (while recognizing the inseparability of these factors). Pedagogical models of redemption are much more open to cultural and religious pluralism, emancipatory struggles, and ecological concerns[27] than are the ransom, substitution, and satisfaction theories that have prevailed in Western theology.[28] The pedagogical model was the earliest of the theories of redemption, and elements of it survived through the patristic period, but then it was lost from view until liberal Protestantism and liberation and feminist theologies rediscovered it. Far from being "weak" or "optimistic," as the standard criticism runs, it is in my opinion the most realistic and intuitively persuasive of any of the theories. It was overwhelmed by a number of counterproductive factors: the domination of kyriarchal, patriarchal structures in the church that submerged the Wisdom motif; the desire of human beings for dramatic rescue and their impatience with the ambiguities of history; the power of the myths of the devil and sacrifice; preoccupation with merit and guilt, reward and punishment, in the juridical paradigm; and the tendency to think of God as accuser and protector (the perennial "rotten points" of religious belief[29]).

In the pedagogical model, Jesus is the Teacher who reveals the true meaning of God and human life and who empowers human beings to discover the truth in their own circumstances and to engage in transformative, emancipatory practices. Here "redemption" does not mean the purchase of freedom (by a ransom, rescue, or sacrifice) but a liberation or emancipation from whatever holds us in bondage (ignorance, superstition, idolatries, ideologies, anxieties, oppressive structures, xenophobias). We must engage in the work of emancipation ourselves; God in Christ empowers us to do so but does not do it for us in any sort of direct, miraculous fashion. God's Wisdom engenders a paideutic process in human history. God may do the teaching, but it is we who must do the learning.

The pedagogical model is not only the truest but also the oldest of the theories of redemption. At the beginning of the second century, the *Didache* and the Apostolic Fathers emphasized what Christ has imparted to us: new knowledge, fresh life, immortality, fellowship with God. He has rescued us from the darkness of error; because of enlightenment received from him, Christians have abandoned idolatry. Christ has made God's Torah known to us and salvation consists in union with him. His sufferings and death do not purchase remission of sins but rather challenge us to repentance. The Apologists, principally Justin Martyr,

stressed that the principal purpose of the incarnation was didactic. J. N. D. Kelly summarizes his view: "Having forgotten the
truth and having been inveigled into ignorance and positive error by the demons, [humans] desperately need the restoration of
the light they have lost." As the new lawgiver, Christ imparts
this saving knowledge; indeed, it was to bestow such illumination or enlightenment that the Logos (Wisdom) became human.
Christ does not merely impart fresh knowledge but also breaks
the spell of the devils who lead humanity astray.[30]

Irenaeus's theory of recapitulation echoed elements of the
pedagogical approach in that what is "recapitulated" in Christ
is the whole history of the formation of the human race through
its loss and recovery of the *imago Dei*. Tertullian, while intro-
ducing the notion of satisfaction, emphasized Christ's achievement as proclaimer of a new law and promise and his role as
"the illuminator and instructor of humankind." Above all, as
we have seen, it was the Alexandrine theologians who developed most fully the idea of Christ as teacher, lawgiver, and
model who endows humans with true knowledge and shows
them the way to salvation. By associating with him, argued
Origen, human beings lose their deadness and irrationality, becoming "divinely possessed and rational." Christ is "the pattern of the perfect life," the exemplar of true virtue into whose
likeness Christians are transformed.[31]

Origen put an interesting spin on the ransom metaphor. It is
not a matter of negotiating with the devil but of outwitting him:
Jesus delivers up his life to the devil in exchange for the release
of human souls, but after accepting the deal the devil discovers
that he cannot hold the Incarnate Lord in his clutches. Thus the
deceiving devil is deceived, outmaneuvered, and done in by
his own devices. Gregory of Nyssa also emphasized that God
defeats evil justly by letting it overextend itself, and Augustine
said in effect that what appears to be a ransom is really a strategy.[32] Demythologized, this has deep insight, for it points to
the way in which evil is actually combated, and redemption actually occurs, in an ambiguous and conflicted world—not by
direct onslaughts of power but by wisdom, by outsmarting

evil, by allowing it enough rope to hang itself. Augustine emphasized not merely this negative strategy but also the exemplary aspect of Christ's work in a way that was without precedent. "Both in his person and in what he has done, Christ, our mediator, has demonstrated God's wisdom and love. The spectacle of such love should have the effect of inciting us to love him in return. . . . More particularly, it should bestir our hearts to adore the humility of God which, as revealed in the incarnation, breaks our pride." This is "the profound mystery (*sacramentum*) by which the bond of sin is broken."[33] All of these ideas reflect the playing-out of Wisdom motifs and the pedagogical model in the history of theology, even when combined with other themes.

A good contemporary representation of this trajectory is John Hick's theory of salvation as human transformation, which he finds to be articulated most profoundly in Eastern Orthodoxy. Salvation occurs through the graduate transformation of human beings into the finite "likeness to God"; this is an assimilation to God (*theosis*) through virtue. While "on the Latin view to be saved is to be justified, i.e. relieved of guilt, by Christ's sacrificial death, on the Orthodox view to be in process of salvation is to be responding to the presence of the divine Spirit and thus gradually moving towards a radical new re-centering within the divine life." He adds that "this Eastern understanding largely coincides with the modern 'liberal' approach initiated in the nineteenth century by Friedrich Schleiermacher." Hick tries to show how Jesus' death fits in with this approach. It is because "an authentic religious leader is willing, if necessary, to be martyred by those who reject the challenging truths that he or she embodies." Indeed, it is because "true prophets and gurus embody, or live out, or incarnate, their teachings that to oppose the message is to oppose the messenger." Thus there is a "tragic appropriateness" to the death of Jesus, as there is to those of Mahatma Gandhi and Martin Luther King Jr. "The voluntary acceptance of death by a holy person has a moral power that reverberates beyond any words that we can frame to express it." Something is happening "that is awe-inspiring and, in an indefinable way, enriching and enhancing to the human community."[34] This shows very clearly how Jesus' crucifixion is, of tragic necessity, part of the divine pedagogy.

Hick believes that salvation construed as human transformation and liberation is an insight that is contained in most of the world's religions, although in quite different forms. Thus, this way of understanding the redemptive work of Christ opens Christianity to interreligious dialogue and avoids both exclusivist and inclusivist claims. The different formulations of salvation are all specifications, Hick proposes, of "the transformation of human existence from self-centeredness to a new orientation centered in the divine Reality."[35] Precisely this is what we have encountered as the fundamental meaning of education from the ancients to the moderns, namely, the drawing of the self out from itself into the whole, the universal, the encompassing, the true. Here the religious and the pedagogical impulses are very close to each other.

Some critics argue that Hick's formulation is overly abstract or generalizing, tending to submerge significant differences in a totalizing scheme. While I believe that the formula offers a deep insight into the character of religion as paideia and paideia as religion, I also acknowledge the risk in using it; for one thing, it is stated in typically Western categories. We must insist, as Hick himself does, that there are many profoundly different and even irreconcilable conceptualizations of what ultimate reality is, but there seems also to be an experience shared widely across cultures that human beings are in some way drawn and shaped by it. Among the "undetermined questions" are whether ultimate reality is knowable or not, whether it is being or nothing, one or many, or the mysterious unity of these contrasts. But these questions need not preclude collaboration and agreement on a broad range of more practical issues.[36]

Divine Wisdom and Human Trans-formation

God's Wisdom becomes "incarnate" not only in Jesus Christ but in every human being who is open and receptive to it. The questions now are how this happens and what role for

Christians Christ may play in this process. How does God's Wisdom work both to *form* human beings and to *transform* and renew them?

We have learned from the philosophical and theological tradition that this process seems to have two basic aspects, which can be described as "immediate" and "mediated." Socrates stressed the element of immediacy, the fact that human beings already know the truth, have it within themselves and need only to recollect it; but at the same time conversation with and stimulus by a teacher are required to elicit it. Thomas Aquinas was clear that an inner light of reason is divinely implanted in every human being, but it remains in potency until it is activated by one's self-discovery or by the instruction of another human person. Calvin emphasized the inner illumination of the Holy Spirit but also recognized that the church must exercise a teaching office rooted in the law, the prophets, the apostles, and above all, Christ.

Hegel constructed a philosophy of Spirit in terms of which it is possible to understand how divine Spirit and human spirit can be inwardly present to each other and mutually actualizing. *Geist* is the whole nexus of spiritual relations: absolute Spirit comes to its own self-consciousness through finite spirit's consciousness of the absolute. From the finite, human side the process has two aspects: on the one hand, religious knowledge is mediated by a pedagogical tradition based on sacred texts and historical revelation (God appears in a concrete human figure); on the other hand, religion is not something that can be mechanically introduced into human beings from without (such as coercing assent to a creed). An external stimulus brings about an internal change, both a recollection of what we know potentially and an organic, spiritual ingestion, an internalizing of what has been given us, making it our own. This ingestion could be regarded as another form of incarnation, of incorporating into our own body something that feeds us, physically or spiritually. Hegel uses the analogy of eating for both education (*Bildung*) and the eucharist.[37] In the case of the latter, there is a physical eating or partaking (*Genuss*) that symbolizes the spiritual incorporation of Christ into the life of the believer. The reason why food can be assimilated is that it is of the same organic substance as the body; thus, by analogy knowledge can be assimilated by human beings and divine Wisdom can bring about human trans-formation because God, humanity, and knowledge/wisdom are of the same spiritual substance.

An interesting version of the distinction between immediacy and mediation is found in the work of the Buddhist Christian scholar Katsumi Takizawa. He argues that there are two kinds of contact between God and human beings. The primary contact is the primordial fact of God with and within us, which lies unconditionally at the foundation of every person's existence. However, this contact often is not known or has been forgotten; hence the need for a secondary contact, an awakening or enlightenment through which a person becomes aware of the primary contact. Enlightenment is the event in which the ego becomes aware of the true Self that is hidden in it. In the case of Jesus and Gotama, the secondary contact was perfectly realized, so that there was an identity between their human egos and their true Selves, the Christ and the Buddha. These perfectly enlightened ones are the means by which enlightenment occurs for others as a mediated reality.[38]

The most profound contemporary articulation of the concept of divine-human mediated immediacy is found, I believe, in the work of Karl Rahner.[39] Divine revelation is possible, he says, because God or absolute being is luminous—sheer luminosity intrinsically self-communicating—and also because human being stands absolutely open to this communication. On the one hand, we cannot say that God's self-revelation has always and everywhere occurred since God is absolutely free and undetermined vis-à-vis humanity and the world. The place where such a revelation may occur is in human history in the form of word—the free word of God made known in human words. We must listen for a revelation in history because we are historical beings. In order to stand before being as such, we must turn toward appearance, that is, the whole of being manifested in the world. Thus there is no unmediated, purely inward and mystical, connection between absolute being and human being; history is the realm of mediation, of communication between Spirit and spirit.

On the other hand, human being as spirit is intrinsically open to absolute Spirit. The transcendental condition that enables the knowing subject to discover that being as such is unlimited, despite the limitedness of all particular objects of knowledge, is our openness to limitlessness. Rahner calls this the *Vorgriff*, the "anticipatory grasp" of all possible objects of knowledge, the "horizon" within which any knowing at all is possible. What is this *Vorgriff*? Toward what does human anticipatory knowing (*vorgreifende Erkennen*) transcend the single object? Is it the absolute being of God, as the perennial philosophy maintained from Plato to Hegel? Or is the horizon within which our objects are conceptually given to us that of sense intuition, which does not reach beyond space and time, as Kant claimed in his critique of metaphysics? Or, finally, does the transcendence that serves as the basis for human existence simply go toward nothingness, as Heidegger concluded? Rahner opts for the perennial philosophy. We do not need to posit a being-toward-nothingness to account for our experience of the finitude of all things. Rather, it is the "Yes" to what is unlimited in itself that makes the negation of the limited possible, not the other way around. It is not "nought that noughtens" but the infinity of being at which the *Vorgriff* aims that unveils the finiteness of all that is immediately given. The "more" of the anticipatory grasp implies an absolute limitlessness of being as such, and thus it opens itself up to a domain beyond spatiotemporal sense intuition. If the grasp is limited to the latter, then it can only aim at nothingness. But the *Vorgriff* toward nothingness is an unverifiable hypothesis and does not adequately describe religious experience. In Rahner's view, Kant already took the critical step toward atheism of which Heidegger is the logical outcome.

Thus the transcendental condition that renders human beings intrinsically open to absolute being is itself absolute being. God is the condition of possibility for knowing God; the link between the infinite and the finite is forged by the infinite, not the finite. However, the anticipatory grasp does not represent the infinite in itself but only co-affirms the infinite as the ultimate whither of the unlimited movement of spirit. Absolute being in and for itself is hidden and not directly cognizable; it is pure light and can be seen only as reflected in finite objects and their negation. Actual knowledge of God occurs when God reveals godself in history, establishing contact, so to speak, with the potential for knowing God that is present within human being as such. This is Rahner's version of the dialectic of mediation and immediacy. The mystical element is present, but it is sublated in the revelatory. In this, Rahner is very close to Hegel.

Perhaps we may venture to suggest that God's Wisdom *forms* human beings in its functioning as the transcendental horizon that draws human beings into the open and enables them to know anything at all, to grow intellectually, to become fully formed persons. But God's Wisdom *transforms* human beings when it occurs as awakening, enlightenment, revelation, when ultimate truth and value are concretely disclosed through a historical mediation. Transformation suggests a change from an unawakened to an awakened condition, from a disoriented life to an oriented one. Orientation requires a sense of purpose and goal, a reorientation from self-centeredness to reality-centeredness. Such reorientation is given from without but appropriated from within. God's Wisdom is at work, mysteriously and profoundly, on both sides of this process.

Whitehead said that the creative impulse toward growth comes from within and is intensely characteristic of each individual. Discovery, discipline, and fruition all come from within. Education works with this impulse, resonates with it, provides it with a larger knowledge and firmer purpose, and guides it toward the most complete achievement of potentialities, which requires an "artistic sense" that subordinates lower to higher possibilities of value. Whitehead acknowledges that this achievement may also entail a religious sensibility, but he understood religion primarily in aesthetic rather than theological terms.

> The ultimate motive power, alike in science, in morality, and in religion, is the sense of value, the sense of importance. It takes the various forms of wonder, of curiosity, of reverence, or worship, of tumultuous desire for merging personality in something beyond itself. This sense of value imposes on life incredible labors, and apart from it life sinks back into the passivity of its lower types. The most penetrating exhibition of this force is the sense of beauty, the aesthetic sense of realized perfection.[40]

Expressed in Christian theological terms, we might say that this "desire for merging personality in something beyond itself" is drawn out and transformed by a revelation of ultimate truth and reality, the most penetrating exhibition of which is the incarnate love of God in Christ, internalized by the witness of the Spirit.

THE PEDAGOGY OF WISDOM: PAIDEIA

The incarnation of Wisdom establishes the determinate forms in which truths and values appear in history. These forms are various because of the inexhaustible mystery of God and the diversity of human experience, but they are not endlessly so and their diversity does not produce a hopeless relativism. A surprisingly small number of great historical-cultural trajectories have become well established; they have withstood the test of time and situation, and they have mediated truth and goodness to generations of human beings (ambiguously mixed, to be sure, with illusion and evil). Of course, the interpretive debates about the meaning of these truths and values are endless. In our own time we are beginning to experience a convergence of the great trajectories and considerable cross-cultural fertilization, which may eventually generate new values and refine old ones. Such is the process of history and of the historical incarnation of God's Wisdom. The transformative power of this Wisdom can become effective in history only when it is thus incarnated in determinate forms. In the preceding section, I considered the form of incarnation central to one religion, Christianity.

In this section, my concern shifts from content to method, from the forms in which Wisdom appears to its pedagogy, its way of engendering teaching and learning. Obviously a connection exists between what is taught and how it is taught. The three elements of the pedagogy of Wisdom identified below certainly reflect the values broadly characteristic of Western culture with its Hebraic, Hellenistic, Christian, and European roots.[41] But as a set of pedagogical skills they do not yield any particular content; rather, they are habits of thinking/imagining/practicing to be brought to bear upon any content, any normative claim, any body of evidence, any array of experience. These elements all have a trans-formative potential and thus they may be gathered under the ancient concept of paideia—the nurturing, forming, and transforming of human beings. Both the content (the incarnation) and the method (the pedagogy) of God's Wisdom are paideutic.

But how adequate is paideia as a model of pedagogy in the modern and postmodern worlds? In his study of theological education, David Kelsey concludes that since the Enlightenment two models of excellence in schooling have confronted each other in an irresolvable tension despite efforts to unify them or negotiate between them. One of these models is paideia in the sense of culturing (*Bildung*), character formation, self-discovery, knowledge in the form of contemplation or insight, engagement with questions of truth, value, and meaning. The other model is science in the sense of *Wissenschaft*, the method of the secular research university for which there can be no claims for truth that are exempt from rigorous critical research. Here observation replaces contemplation, and questions about truth and meaning tend to be avoided: we can trust what we see with our empirical, physical vision, but not with our intuitive, spiritual vision. Kelsey describes the contrast metaphorically as one between "Athens," the seat of ancient wisdom, and "Berlin," the first of the modern research universities.[42]

This conflict certainly exists and is unlikely to diminish: it is what lies behind the tension between religious studies (modeled on the "scientific" paradigm) and theological studies (as paideutic); and within theological education it appears as the tension between an emphasis on "understanding God truly" and on preparing persons for church leadership. Perhaps the best that can be done, as Kelsey recommends, is to negotiate between the two models and maintain a truce, or balance. However, I do not believe that the conflict is logically entailed by either paideia or *Wissenschaft*. Hegel developed a conception of *Wissenschaft* that is broad enough to include contemplative or speculative knowledge as its highest moment. The science of knowledge—*Wissenschaft* in the sense of *scientia*—must of necessity include all forms of knowledge or consciousness, ranging from the sentient, psychic, empirical, analytic, and social to the aesthetic, religious, and speculative. Philosophy as a whole is "the science (*Wissenschaft*) of the experience of consciousness," and the "encyclopedia of the philosophical sciences (*Wissenschaften*)" culminates in the knowledge of God as absolute truth and being.[43] Hegel's dialectical method comprises the elements of immediate experience, critical reflection, and encompassing vision. Ironically, the preeminent Berlin philosopher of the early nineteenth century developed a concept of *Wissenschaft* that did not conflict with the paideia of Athens, but his way did not prevail and it is impossible to retrieve it today.

It is more promising in my judgment to approach the task of integration from the side of paideia, recognizing that those who are principally oriented to the paradigm of the research university and empirical science are unlikely to be persuaded by it. Paideia includes a commitment to critical, disciplined research, as rigorous as anything demanded by the university, but it brings this commitment into play with other elements that are just as important: contemplation, insight, imagination, affections, practices. It seeks to integrate these in terms of an inclusive vision of wisdom as its paideutic goal, which is the fullest possible actualization of the human potential in each and every person. Implicit in this actualization, I believe, is the

knowledge and love of God (or of ultimate truth, reality, goodness), but this knowledge remains the indirect rather than the
direct object of most education.

Caution, however, is advised. Kelsey points out that the two
models, paideia and *Wissenschaft*, or wisdom and science, not
only entail different institutional arrangements and distinctive
conceptions of their subject matter; they also presuppose, he
suggests, "two very different and, in some respects incompatible, anthropologies."[44] One of these anthropologies understands human being as "spirit in the world," to use Karl
Rahner's expression, while the other approaches the human as
a highly complex material phenomenon. Any attempt at integration today will privilege one or another of these anthropologies (with their accompanying worldviews), and it is difficult
to imagine how they both could be equally true, or how either
could do full justice to the other. We continue to live in the clash
of cultures generated by these anthropologies, and an overarching synthesis of the Hegelian kind would require cultural
conditions that no longer (or do not yet again) obtain. Paideutic integration assumes something like Hegel's broad way of
understanding "science" (*Wissenschaft*), which is not widely
shared by present-day natural and social science. Yet attempts
at negotiation, compromise, and ad hoc integration are needed
to prevent the cultural clash from becoming more destructive
of human well-being than it already is. And there is evidence
of openness to such efforts on the part of those searching for a
new scientific paradigm.

Paideia as the pedagogy of Wisdom comprises, in the proposal that follows, three fundamental elements: *critical thinking,
heightened imagination,* and *liberating practice.* These correspond,
in slightly different form, to the elements of the rhythm of education I discussed in chapter 3: imagination (romance), discipline (precision), and freedom (generalization, fruition). They
are individually connected with other elements of the transformative pedagogy I discussed in that chapter: critical thinking
with constructive and interactive knowledge, heightened imagination with connected teaching, and liberating practice with

education as the practice of freedom. Other scholars have arrived at a similar designation of pedagogical elements,[45] and thus I am encouraged that my approach is not entirely arbitrary or idiosyncratic. In fact, it is rather traditional in the sense that the elements correspond to cognitive, aesthetic, and ethical dimensions of human experience. What I am calling "God's Wisdom" appears as a depth dimension or transformative power within each of these elements, marked by the adjectival qualifiers "critical," "heightened," and "liberating."

Critical Thinking

Paideia entails a multidimensional critical thinking. On the broadest horizon it appears as what Edward Farley calls "meta-method" or "meta-field" thinking. This is a thinking of the being, truth, and reality of things at a level of awareness unobtainable simply by technical methods. Each of the disciplinary fields has its own distinctive type of thinking, its way of awakening and engaging its subject matter, which is often hidden beneath its research methods and rarely, if ever, discussed. Thus one of the critical tasks of paideia as meta-field thinking is to think the fields of thinking. Meta-field thinking is oriented to "the unstable, ever self-transcending concreteness of what is actual," and thus it corrects the abstractions that serve the methodological requirements of a discipline; its task is to "destabilize the apparently fixed success" of research methods, and "resynthesize what focused research has fragmented." It attends to the *Sache,* or subject matter illumined by a specialty field, which functions as a kind of cognitive horizon within which every concrete object of research subsists. By reflecting on the *Sache* of a field, one deconstructs the field itself in the sense that its "horizonal character, unvoiced perspectives, selectivity of methods, and fuzzy and interdependent boundaries with other fields" are all exposed.[46]

In addition to meta-field thinking, there are various intrafield thinkings from which the critical methods that constitute the disciplines of the research university arise. It is important to emphasize that these too belong to paideia, which is not opposed to *Wissenschaft* in the broad sense of the sciences and scholarly methods of the academic world, for the latter contribute powerfully to the formation and flourishing of human beings. Without them, there would be no advance in technical knowledge, no empirically established information about nature, psyche, and culture, no lasting intellectual accomplishments. Rigorous disciplining in the traditions, methods, and problems of a research field is necessary for anyone who wishes to contribute to scholarship. At the same time, the in-depth concentration required of a research regimen can produce a myopia that blots out awareness of other methods and other constructions of reality. Our culture generally has an oversupply of narrowly trained experts and fewer and fewer well-educated persons who manifest the wisdom of seeing things whole.

Some of the elements of critical thinking at both the metafield and intra-field level have been discussed in chapter 3: the dialectical, dialogical, and relational character of thinking; critical scrutiny of conventional beliefs as well as of one's own presuppositions and interests; awareness that all knowledge is both constructed and interactive; the distinctive blend of detachment and engagement, skepticism and commitment, that is present in critical reflection. Charles Anderson identifies the following steps in the cultivation of reason, which he regards as central to the function of a university: mastery of basic skills, discernment and critique of one's own performance and that of others, judgment by which one recognizes that it is possible to think otherwise about a matter, awareness of relativity, development of creativity and innovation, and engagement with transcendence (the ultimate questions of meaning, context, and purpose).[47] These steps correspond to some degree with the forms of intellectual development identified by William Perry. The critical thinking movement that is currently popular in colleges has as its basic premises the ideas that critical thinking originates in the learner's engagement with problems, principally through writing, and that it consists of two central activities that are generic across all disciplines: identifying and challenging assumptions, and exploring alternative ways of thinking and acting through dialogic exchanges.[48]

My theological premise is that God's Wisdom evokes human thinking and demands that it be *radically critical*. Such criticism cuts (*krinein*) to the very root (*radix*) of thinking itself, engendering on the one hand an awareness of thinking's fundamentally gratuitous character as a power given to us that enables us to connect with the ultimate mystery of things; and on the other hand an acknowledgment of the limits, self-interest, illusion, and folly that are ever-present in human wisdom. Such critical judgment of reason implies a perspective that transcends human reason without cancelling it, namely, revelation, which is the divine rationality. Reason, the power of thinking, is the glory of God in humanity, yet it is also the source of enormous human misery. What is needed is its redemption and reorientation, not its diminution or displacement. The only thing powerful enough to fight the evil caused by reason is reason itself. The goal is a communicative, liberating rationality, a critical thinking turned away from self-centeredness to reality-centeredness.[49]

Heightened Imagination

Imagination represents the contemplative, intuitive, visionary, and affective elements of paideia. It powerfully expresses the aspect of "seeing" that is present in wisdom. Seeing involves vision and images, and it binds together the mental and the physical. Physical sight requires the activity of mind, and intellectual vision or intuition expresses itself metaphorically through a wealth of physical imagery. Human beings are thinking beings only as embodied in the world, and this embodiment affects every facet of their thinking. For too long education has treated minds as though they were disembodied or disincarnate, and today the role of the body in education is a topic of considerable discussion.[50]

This is the approach emphasized by Maria Harris in her suggestive work *Teaching and Religious Imagination*.[51] Imaginative teaching, she writes, "is the incarnation of subject matter in ways that lead to the revelation of subject matter." In this process persons discover themselves as "possessing grace of power, especially the power of re-creation, not only of themselves, but of the world in which they live." Imagination expresses itself in teaching through five principal moments, or dance-like steps: contemplation, engagement, formgiving, emergence, and release. Harris defines each of her key terms as follows: *Imagination* is the power to change, reverse, re-create reality, the power to shape into one (*Einbildungskraft*) as understood by Kant and Coleridge. *Religion* is a way of valuing that attends to mystery, the numinous, the mystical; and in its root sense of binding together (*re-ligio*) it is very close to the assimilative power of imagination. Thus religion is intrinsically imaginative in its expressions, and imagination is at heart religious. The ultimate subject matter of teaching as an act of religious imagination is "a Creator divinity, always acting in human affairs, holding all being by its sacred presence, . . . the Subjectivity of subjectivity," the One in which and in whom everything and everyone participates.

Contemplation, according to Harris, means seeing what is there, and it occurs in the co-presence of teacher, student, subject matter, and environment. *Engagement* means diving in, wrestling with, and rolling around in the subject matter; it is contemplation brought to bear on something tangible. *Formgiving* is the incarnation of subject matter, giving it body, form, flesh. Teaching is a constant creation of forms—verbal forms, earth forms, embodied forms, and forms of discovery. *Emergence* is the point where something new is born and the learner takes possession of it. *Release* is letting the new form go forth, sending it into the world, where it will take on a life of its own. It is also the return into a new moment of contemplation so that the round may continue in a never-ending cycle. *Revelation* means that the teacher does not bring the subject matter but re-creates it in the student by helping the student to know what he or she already potentially knows. The revelation of subject matter is directed toward the formation of the divine image, which can never be seen directly or fully. This image gives a *grace of power* that leads to communion and issues in a tranformative praxis whose goal is a *re-creation* of the world in accord with love and justice.

Harris's version of imagination is quite explicitly religious, and, while I find myself affirming and being instructed by what she says, I recognize that imagination is a quality that ideally is present in all aspects of teaching and learning, not just those aspects engaged with religious material. In this respect I believe that Bernard Meland's identification of the "appreciative consciousness" provides a helpful resource. The appreciative consciousness is essentially imaginative and affective in character, and it, together with the rational consciousness and the moral consciousness, opens up the dimension of "spirit." The term "spirit," while not entirely satisfactory, writes Meland, "connotes a quality of human discernment which embraces the goods of the ethical, the intellectual, and the aesthetic life," and "it holds these concerns together as inseparable facets of the human spirit."[52]

Meland's theory has been developed out of resources provided by William James, Henry Nelson Wieman, and Alfred North Whitehead. The appreciative consciousness, as he defines it, is "an orientation of the mind which makes for a maximum degree of receptivity to the datum under consideration on the principle that what is given may be more than what is immediately perceived, or more than one can think." It can also be called intellectual humility, wonder, reverence, open awareness. It is evoked by the recognition that the actual is always pointing beyond itself to what is possible and hidden. There is an element of inexhaustibility in every experienced event, accompanied by a sense of expectancy, knowing that creativity is occurring. A second step beyond receptivity is the act of identification with what is given, sharing to some degree the feeling-content of an object: feeling is "the wisdom of the body." A third step is discrimination, the act of noting the vivifying contrasts that differentiate the datum and set it apart as distinctive. These three aspects—receptivity, identification, and discrimination— are often associated with an aesthetic and poetic temperament, but they must, Meland believes, be incorporated into the educational project as a whole. Appreciation nurtures capacities such as empathy and sensitivity, and it helps people turn from self-centeredness to reality-centeredness. Religion without the appreciative consciousness can "degenerate into a pathological concern for salvation from sin," losing "the envisagement of a good not our own, the beauty of holiness, the glory of God."[53]

My theological premise is that God's Wisdom evokes human imagination and demands that it be *radically heightened* (and *deepened*). This heightening/deepening means an acute attunement to what is presenting itself in the actual. It is a seeing that sees through the phenomenal into the mystical, knowing that the mystical cannot be seen; it sees the glory of God reflected in the glory of creation, and the suffering of God in the agony of creation. It does not divert attention from the real; rather, it seeks "the mystery beneath the real."[54] It gives to our eyes, in the words of Coleridge, "a magnifying power," emancipated from "the black shapeless accidents of size."[55] Such heightening/deepening/magnifying implies that a revelatory, disclosive power is at work in human imagination—as it was in Jesus' parabolic envisagement of the realm of God.

Liberating Practice

While there is an aspect of education that glories in knowledge for the sake of knowledge, and beauty for the sake of beauty, the basic orientation of paideia, concerned as it is with the formation of human beings, is toward the good and the practice of the good. This ancient Socratic insight, found also in the praxis-oriented teaching of Jesus, has been rearticulated by postmodern pedagogy: education is for the sake of the practice of freedom. Freedom is the principal form in which the good seems to appear for an age in which the consciousness of both bondage and liberation has been heightened. To flourish, we believe, human beings must be free, but the subtle intricacies of oppression have been exposed as never before. We find ourselves engaged in an endless and seemingly unwinnable struggle for the good.

At this point it will help to remind ourselves that in the case of education we are in for the long haul—long in a cultural sense as well as an individual one. The cultivation of practical reason is indeed possible, fruitful, and unending. Teachers and students can examine a pattern of practice, criticize it with an eye to its improvement, and distinguish between excellence and error. Good practices can be taught, but they are not necessarily learned, and if learned they will be forgotten.[56] Education is never finished.

None of this is dramatic and glamorous, and it has been at the heart of liberal education for two-and-a-half millennia. The purpose of a liberal education, says Martha Nussbaum, is "to produce free citizens, citizens who are free not because of wealth or birth, but because they can call their minds their own." Such persons will not be uncritical moral relativists, but they will recognize that the struggle for moral truth and goodness is unending. Democracy requires citizens with the strength of mind and heart to endure in this struggle. Education for freedom is both enriched and complicated today by the plurality of cultures, traditions, and values to which teachers and students are increasingly exposed. Despite or perhaps because of this, Nussbaum reports discovering an astonishing variety of creative proposals for carrying forward the project of liberal and liberating education in today's colleges and universities. Yet everywhere teachers and students struggle to keep going under tough conditions resulting from ideological opposition, cost-cutting, and a strong emphasis on vocational studies.[57]

One of my concerns is to establish a connection between the liberal and liberating traditions. Liberal education and liberal theology have often emphasized freedom of thought and conviction without attending sufficiently to an analysis and transformation of the social conditions that determine who has the freedom to think and what the connections are between knowledge and power. In my judgment this is a false dichotomy: the Enlightenment project of intellectual freedom is not complete without the social and cultural practices of freedom to which postmodern pedagogy attends. Conversely, projects of liberation and social transformation need the Enlightenment legacy of rigorous, self-critical reflection. Nussbaum certainly recognizes these connections: she proposes to open up the Western canon

and to reform liberal education in the direction of cultural pluralism and engagement with the experience of ethnic minorities
and women.[58]

Recent discussions of theological education have emphasized
the centrality of practice, and of liberating practice in particular.
All theology is ultimately practical, argues Craig Dykstra, properly oriented to the identification, study, and pursuit of practices
that are constitutive of Christian faith and life.[59] Don Browning
believes that all theology is "fundamental practical theology" in
the sense of "critical reflection on the church's dialogue with
Christian sources and other communities with the aim of guiding its action toward social and individual transformation."
Practical philosophy emphasizes the importance of *phronēsis,*
practical wisdom, understood as critical reflection about the
goals of human action, which should guide the interpretive
process from the beginning. Instead of a theory-to-practice (text-
to-application) model, it offers a practice-theory-practice model,
which Browning proposes to apply to the structure of theological studies.[60] Rebecca Chopp works this out most concretely in
her recent study of theological education. Theology, she argues,
is "saving work," which "offers a material vision and an embodied wisdom for a new form of Christianity." Saving work engages in practices that are fundamentally emancipatory, and it
demands a form of knowing that is transformative. Chopp applies a pragmatic theory of rhetoric as the principal means of engendering emancipatory practices that have as their goal
"planetary and human flourishing."[61]

My theological premise is that God's Wisdom evokes such
practices and demands that they be *radically liberating.* The radical character of liberation is connected with the fact that "the
creation itself will be set free from its bondage to decay and will
obtain the freedom of the glory of the children of God" (Rom.
8:21). Freedom is the image of God in humanity, but it is an ex-
ceedingly fragile quality, in continual need of liberation from
whatever constrains it. Freedom can be diminished by the loss
of consciousness of it as well as by physical bondage, psychological wounding, and socioeconomic oppression. The practice
of freedom entails a radically new logic, a reversal of the logic

of power, domination, self-interest, reward and punishment, that characterizes the everyday world. It is a logic of grace, giving, opening, relating, which is always being pushed to the margins of the established economies. Yet without freedom human beings cannot flourish. It is the greatest gift of education, but in the final analysis education does not give it but evokes it, calls it forth from within. These paradoxes indicate that in the case of freedom we are dealing with something that is radical and mysterious, something at the heart of God's Wisdom.[62]

The three elements that comprise the pedagogy of Wisdom—critical thinking, heightened imagination, and liberating practice—should not be presumed to occur in this or any other sequential order. Each presupposes and triggers the other in a rhythmic process. Something must drive human beings into critical thinking in the first place, and this can be understood to be imagination in the form of romance—the eros, hunger, passion to know the world and to wonder at both its inexhaustible wealth and its tragic conflicts. (As my flight companion intuitively expressed it, there is something truly "wonderful" about teaching and learning.) We are also driven to know by the need to act, by the recognition that we are always already engaged with human beings in their vulnerable otherness and cannot avoid making complex ethical decisions. Critical thinking in turn yields a higher form of imagination, an aesthetic appreciation of what gives itself in the breadth and depth of the real; and thinking finds its fulfillment in practices oriented to the good, to freedom. But what *are* "the good" and "freedom"? Emancipatory practices demand critical theories. So the three elements are interrelated in a dialectical spiral, which is neither circular nor linear.

In reflecting back over this chapter, I want to emphasize that what I propose here is not a theology of Christian or religious education but a Christian theology of education as such and as a whole. The chapter takes on a Christian cast by attending to the incarnation of God's Wisdom in Jesus of Nazareth, and I argue that Jesus provides a distinctive, indeed radical model of a redemptive or transformative pedagogy that has not lost its power for nearly two millennia. God's Wisdom must of necessity become incarnate if it is to be redemptively efficacious in human history, but there are a multitude of such incarnations, none of which can claim exclusive or final validity. Jesus is a *paradigm* of incarnation, not the sole incarnation.

From a Christian perspective whose relativity and limits are freely acknowledged, my claim is that God's Wisdom is the ultimate source and telos of all human education. Following Karl Rahner, I have suggested that this Wisdom constitutes the transcendental horizon that draws human beings into knowledge. Without this *Vorgriff*, this anticipatory grasp, human beings would be unable to pull themselves out of immediacy and self-absorption into an engagement with the real. And without the historical appearance or revelation of God's Wisdom through a variety of cultural mediations and mediators such as Christ, knowledge of goodness, truth, beauty, love, freedom would not be possible. The same conclusion might be argued from a Jewish perspective in terms suggested by Martin Buber and Emmanuel Levinas: human beings can get outside themselves into an engagement with the real only if something wrenches them away from self-preoccupation—and it is the ethical sphere that accomplishes this in and through the face of the other.[63] The face of the other mediates the infinite Other, for the human other partakes of infinity and can never be reduced to the same (*my* same). Thus the ethical relationship in which this e-duction occurs implies a religious dimension, a reference to an encompassing Other in whom all finite others are preserved and connected. This Jewish way of looking at the matter is not incompatible with Christianity, especially when Jesus' being-for-others even unto death is emphasized. This way of thinking is remarkably close in certain respects to the self-emptying of Buddhism—an emptying that is also a filling, an enlightening, a taking-up of a new way of knowing and being in the world. That is what makes education transformative. Viewed in Jewish and Christian perspective, such education is the work of God's Wisdom, which encounters us in a diversity of incarnate forms, inspires us from within, claims us in the other, and draws us out of ourselves into the free and open.

5

Conclusion

Paideia in Higher Education Today

Our discussion thus far has been mostly theoretical. An obvious question is whether what has been said will prove to have any "cash value" for the complex questions facing higher education today. Before I attempt to address this matter, it may be helpful to summarize the argument that has developed to this point. Theologically, my claim is that God's Wisdom engenders, both outwardly through its incarnate shapes and inwardly through the illumination of the Spirit, a distinctive sort of wisdom in human beings. To name this wisdom and describe its pedagogical characteristics, I have adopted the ancient term paideia (the association of wisdom and paideia has the advantage of bringing together the Hebraic and Greek heritages of Christian theology). Education as paideia is, in the most fundamental sense, nurturing or formative of human life; without it, human beings can scarcely exist as human at all, and they certainly cannot flourish. Education as paideia also has a rhythmic quality that includes three basic elements related to one another cyclically. One of these is critical, disciplined thinking, which constitutes objects of investigation through various methodological procedures, but which also finds itself drawn dialogically into the mystery of thinking and being as such. It knows itself as thinking to be both constructive and connected. A second element surrounds critical thinking. Initially it is a precritical, immediate, romantic engagement with what presents itself in experience. Later it becomes a postcritical contemplation, appreciation, and appropriation of critically constructed reality and of the mystery that runs through it—an imaginative seeing of the whole in the parts and the parts in the whole. The third element is that of fruition, synthesis, commitment, freedom—an envisagement of the good that incorporates both cognitive and aesthetic aspects and is oriented toward transformative, liberating practices. God's Wisdom appears as a transcendent dimension or radicalizing power within each of these elements, drawing criticism to its depths, imagination to its heights, and practice to its telos in freedom.

The basic purpose of education is to awaken, discipline, focus, and expand the development of wisdom in human beings as they respond in however diverse ways to the beckoning call of being, truth, goodness. If awareness of the latter is repressed, it needs to be released, brought into the open, and connected with other elements in the educational experience. This is the religious dimension that is for the most part silently present in all forms of education. One of my convictions is that the practice of paideia is pretty much the same across the broad spectrum of higher education. That is, the elements of critical thinking, heightened imagination, and liberating practice, together with their religious implications, are or should be always present in the great diversity of levels, subject matters, methods, and professional orientations. How they concretely appear, in whatever distinctive combinations and emphases, will differ tremendously. But a common thread links the practice of education wherever and however it appears. This at least is my thesis. I shall examine it by looking first at liberal education in general and then at religious and theological studies in particular. I select the latter because it is my own field and because I lack the expertise to test the thesis in other disciplines. I hope this limitation does not overly prejudice the case.

PAIDEIA IN LIBERAL EDUCATION

At the end of the previous chapter I noted that according to Martha Nussbaum the goal of liberal education is "to produce free citizens, citizens who are free not because of wealth or birth, but because they can call their minds their own." This is an education that is truly "fitted for freedom" (the classical meaning of *liberalis*). It is for everyone, not just males of the propertied classes as was the case from ancient times right up to the beginning of the twentieth century. Nussbaum believes that American higher education comes closer to this ideal, with its commitment to "a core of common studies that is regarded as essential to the good life for each and every person," than does European education with its division into humanistic and vocational tracks at the beginning of secondary schooling.

Liberal education strives for two further ideals, according to Nussbaum: it should be suited to individual students' circumstances and context, and it should be pluralistic, concerned with a variety of norms and traditions. The pluralistic ideal by no means entails a cultural and moral relativism that holds all ways of life and all values to be equally good. Rather, judgments about ways of life and values are arrived at through criticism and dialogue. Finally, Nussbaum believes that the emphasis of a liberal education should fall on thinking rather than on learning things from (great) books. "There is no substitute for thinking things through, and the hope for a quick fix for complicated problems" by finding answers in books will dissipate. "We live in a messy, puzzling, and complicated world, in which there is absolutely no substitute for one's own active searching."[1]

Nussbaum is encouraged about the state of higher education in America today. "Never before have there been so many talented and committed young faculty so broadly dispersed in institutions of so many different kinds, thinking about difficult issues connecting education with citizenship," struggling "to reason well about urgent questions and to engage the hearts and minds of their students in that search."[2] She acknowledges that at the same time severe problems persist, reflected in the scarcity of full-time teaching positions, institutional cost-cutting, and the prevalence of a corporate mentality among administrators and a vocational mentality among students. But, on the whole, she is optimistic.

Others do not share her optimism. Bruce Wilshire paints a gloomy picture in his book, *The Moral Collapse of the University.*

He wonders where questions about truth, goodness, and reality get addressed when scholarly research has become so disconnected from teaching, and he fears that the university as a whole, as a vital unit, is disappearing into its component parts. Wilshire charges that scholarly disciplines engage in "purification rituals" by which they distinguish themselves as insiders from outsiders who lack expertise, and a pervasive alienation is felt by both students and faculty. Science and technology, professionalism and bureaucracy, have led to the "drifting belief that we cannot achieve meaning and truth about the human condition as a whole, that we can tell no life-forming story about what we are and what we ought to be that is compatible with truth."[3] Wilshire's prescription is to reorganize the university on a human scale where students and faculty would be personally present to each other and where good teaching would in fact be as highly regarded as good research. This might be accomplished by creating a number of small undergraduate colleges within a university whose purpose would be "to promote liberal, that is, liberating education, . . . which frees from constricting prejudices and ideologies" and promotes the flourishing of personhood. Faculty within a college would teach across disciplinary partitions. In place of the patriarchal pyramid by which universities are organized, Wilshire offers the image of the "Neolithic circle" around which persons and ideas freely flow.[4] What this might mean in terms of specific organizational structures he does not explain.

Charles Anderson strikes a posture somewhere between Nussbaum and Wilshire. He agrees with Nussbaum that universities in a liberal democracy should attempt to *shape* thought and conscience, not simply stand for freedom of thought and conscience in a value-neutral environment. Values must be taught and assessed, but how? For this we must have some sense of the moral purpose of the university and its goals, but it is just this sense that has largely collapsed (here he agrees with Wilshire). Scholars hesitate to make judgments beyond their own narrow specialties, and the reigning ideology is one of tolerance or more precisely of mutual indifference: "I'll let you

alone if you let me alone."[5] Anderson tells the story of how this
came about. The aim of the research universities that began to
appear at the end of the nineteenth century was no longer the
cultivation of (Christian) character, as had been the case with the
(religiously affiliated) liberal arts colleges out of which many of
them evolved; rather, their aim was the production of knowledge, achieved by organizing and rationalizing the processes of
discovery. The university became a knowledge factory made up
of specialized research disciplines; its aim was not truth or wisdom but analytic power. Researchers replaced sages. Basically
the university today is an administrative arrangement, a holding
company for organized disciplines, itself empty of philosophy
and operating on a market model of production with little collective responsibility. The educated person is a detached, often
cynical, ironic observer of the random interplay of forces.[6]

Anderson's proposed philosophy for determining the purpose of the university is a pragmatic liberalism that yields a theory of practical reason. The central criteria here are rational
discourse and communication, open inquiry, right proportion
or fairness, political and economic justice, and human freedom.
Achievement of these goals requires critical analysis, judgment,
creativity and innovation, and a willingness to address ultimate
questions of meaning, context, and purpose—or, in a single
word, "wisdom."[7] Anderson makes the important point that *access to wisdom is through the disciplines,* not around them or apart
from them. The disciplines should be seen not as ends in themselves but as instruments for the development of mind and
spirit.[8] Thus his proposal for curricular reorganization is pragmatic in the sense that it works with the existing disciplines and
attempts to draw them into a collaborative undertaking. Rather
than defining a core curriculum, Anderson identifies core elements *of* a curriculum: civilization (not enculturation in a specific tradition but orientation of students to the whole process of
education and the disciplines of mind), natural sciences, the human situation (social sciences), the humanities, practical (pre-
vocational) studies, and practical philosophy (political, moral,
scientific).[9] Although he recognizes a religious dimension in

education, Anderson does not seem to give it a specific place in his curriculum, thematized on its own account.[10]

It is at this point that I find the proposal of Denise Lardner Carmody intriguing. Writing explicitly from the point of view of a Catholic Christian theology of higher education, she asks what difference the idea of God might make in one's view of education. It will entail, she says, a radical freedom from idols and tyrants and a shift in perspective from worldly wisdom to divine Wisdom. Everything is the same yet different in the light of this Wisdom. Theology of education legitimates all human inquiry and affirms full academic freedom, but it offers a different view of human destiny, based on grace and the gift of freedom.[11] Carmody identifies four main areas (or "zones of reality") of a comprehensive liberal arts curriculum: human nature, physical nature, politics (the social realm), and divinity (the religious realm). The pursuit of wisdom reveres the whole, the universe, the development of human potential in all of these areas. The educational sin against the Holy Spirit is parochialism; by contrast, college education must be broad and deep. Students should become acquainted with major realms of knowledge and with both the vast differences and deep similarities in cultures.[12]

Divinity or religion/theology, in this radical proposal, deserves equal attention in the curriculum with the other main areas. The study of divinity addresses the awareness of the unbounded, the divine mystery, at the core of all human civilizations, the radical source of human being and human liberation. Divinity is immanent in the other curricular zones, and it helps to make the multiversity into a university. It enlarges our sense of mind and requires us to attend to the whole, which can never be mastered. Carmody's curriculum would require of every student six courses in divinity on two tracks, one for Christian students (starting with scripture, doctrine, ethics/spirituality), the other for non-Christian ones (starting with biblical studies, world religions, contemplation/action).[13] Beyond this would be a number of more focused courses for majors and electives. "In their six courses in divinity, students would be expected to grapple long and hard (and deeply!) with the significance of God," with agnosticism and atheism, with the faiths of other world religions, and in general with a striving for the wisdom and holiness that are essential to becoming mature human beings.[14]

Obviously this is a proposal that would be acceptable today only in a religiously affiliated college, but I am impressed by its seriousness and rigor. If the religious dimension of education is as important as I have been arguing, then it cannot be treated casually in one or two survey courses or subsumed as an element of other disciplines. It must be studied in its own right as an essential ingredient of a liberal arts curriculum. If we wish to have well-educated lay people who can contribute something of substance to religious institutions and to society as a whole, and who have a sense of the meaning, value, and orientation of human life, it will take something like this by way of systematic, ordered learning in the great religious traditions to accomplish the goal. This idea seems like a utopian dream, yet with will and determination it could be accomplished.

Making divinity an equal partner in liberal arts education, along with humanistic studies, social studies, and the natural sciences, offers an opportunity, writes Carmody, "to form students toward wisdom. Teachers cannot make students wise. For wisdom, experience and the Spirit of God are the key factors." But professors can orient students so that they will long for wisdom and continue seeking it the rest of their lives. The proper end of education, as of the course of life, is the divine mystery. "The mental horizon that allows us to scan the world, and the sense of self that allows us to wonder at the ineffable aspects of human creativity, comes from the presence of God in our awareness—from the company of God as the tacit 'other' and partner in all that we do." The heart of education may be expressed in Irenaeus's axiom that "the glory of God is human beings made fully alive" (*gloria Dei vivens homo*).[15] Pedagogically, this means that God works in the world toward the fullest human capacity to think and act responsibly. As such, God is not the direct but the indirect object/subject of all education.

As I have said, this is a strong proposal that has virtually no chance of being adopted by a secular university. But it could be implemented by a religiously affiliated institution, whose mission should certainly not be that of indoctrinating students in its own tradition and creed (the educational sin of parochialism!) but of exposing them to the full range of human religious experience, critically, appreciatively, and with an orientation to practice. Indeed, Martha Nussbaum makes this very point. Religious universities, she says, should have love of neighbor at their heart in a special way, knowing that love is at the center of every major religion, that ignorance is a great enemy of love, and that education in diversity is a necessary weapon against ignorance. It is for reasons such as these that the major religions have founded universities, believing that love at its best is intelligent and that higher education can enhance its discrimination.[16] In fulfilling its religious mission, such a university would also be fulfilling its mission to liberal education, perhaps even more adequately than its secular counterparts. As for the latter, while religious studies would not have as central a role, they can still be present, and the general paideutic goal of nurturing wisdom and love can still be affirmed.

PAIDEIA IN RELIGIOUS AND THEOLOGICAL STUDIES

The approach to liberal education described above casts the discussion of religious and theological studies into a somewhat different light. If the goal of liberal education as a whole is to nurture wisdom and love, enhance appreciation, and encourage practices of freedom and justice, then the differences between religious studies and theological studies cannot be as sharp as they are often represented to be. These differences began to emerge when religious studies was widely established as a university discipline in public institutions in the 1960s, following a Supreme Court ruling that distinguished between the practice and teaching *of* religion and teaching *about* religion. The latter was judged to be permissible in publicly funded schools, and new departments of religious studies were eager to demonstrate that they were just as objective and rigorously scientific as other university disciplines. There was no place for "theology" in the religious studies curriculum if theology meant, as was widely assumed, a confessional embrace of and advocacy for specific doctrinal truth claims.

This was a recipe for an unproductive and unnecessary conflict between the ideals of paideia and science. Religious studies has certainly made tremendous advances in bringing a variety of methodological tools to bear on the study of religious traditions: historical, comparative, sociological, anthropological, psychological, literary, linguistic, cultural, and so forth. We have never known more about religion, but it seemed to be tacitly assumed that this wealth of information was of little relevance for the lives and convictions of students; or at least its relevance should not be directly discussed. Thus, as Edward Farley has pointed out, religious studies relieved itself of the responsibility of addressing and assessing the wisdom of specific communities of faith. The very thing that a religion is most fundamentally about—its insight into the nature of reality—is bracketed, not engaged critically and empathetically. "Utter existential indifference to the truths posed by or laid claim to in the subject matter," writes Farley, "is a deadly virus, a virtual AIDS of education."[17] At the same time, theology became ghettoized, restricted to the wisdom internal to a specific community of faith, of which it was presumed to be an uncritical advocate. The effect of both of these trends is fideism. If religion is taught only phenomenally and descriptively, its contents cannot be appraised and appropriated. Faith becomes a more or less arbitrary, private matter, relying on personal experience and confessional authorities that are not subject to public, rational scrutiny.[18]

Both religious studies and theological studies are valid paradigms; while different from each other, they need not conflict with each other.[19] The distinction between "teaching *of*" and "teaching *about*" religion must be regarded as a partial truth, useful for legal purposes, but finally not persuasive since one of the things taught "about" a religion is precisely its own distinctive claims and insights. What is intended to be excluded here are indoctrination, dogmatism, and parochialism, but these are as much the bane of theology as they are of liberal studies in general. Religious and theological studies share more in common than what distinguishes them. In my view, each must be included as a necessary moment within the other. From a religious studies perspective, with its primary emphasis on critical analysis and comparative description, there must be a moment when specific religions are interpreted as faiths with their reality claims. The interpretation of faith requires entering into the hermeneutic modes constituting that faith, and this entails theological reflection, an appreciation of and participation in the realities that are presenting themselves. It is possible to enter empathetically into a reality-construal that is not one's own, to experience its power and think its thoughts, imagining what it would be like to see things from this point of view, adopting as an outsider the insider's perspective. If one restricts oneself to a religion's external forms of expression and cultural functions, then the thing it is all about has not been fully understood.

From a theological studies perspective, with its primary emphasis on understanding, appreciation, engagement, and practice, there must also be a rigorously critical moment, a distanciation that precedes the appropriation (as Paul Ricoeur says), a movement as an insider to the outsider's perspective. Otherwise the appropriation will not be *theological* but simply the act of faith itself. At this point the critical methods of religious studies are of great benefit to theology. They enhance and deepen the theologian's understanding of religion, of its psychological dynamics, of how it has arisen and how it functions in human cultures, of what its corrupt, or "rotten," points are, of its potential for both good and evil. If theology is to be a *critical* as opposed to a dogmatic engagement with, and rethinking of, the truth and reality claims of a specific religious faith, then it must incorporate this *wissenschaftlich* element within itself. If religious studies is to bring its students into a life-enriching *engagement* with its materials as opposed to a deadly historicism, it must incorporate a paideutic element within itself. Religious and theological studies seem to come together at the point of *critical engagement,* which is present in both of them in different ways—paideia within science, and science within paideia. They share the objective common to liberal education of nurturing wisdom and love in human beings.

A similar approach to the integration of religious and theological studies is set forth by David Ford in the inaugural issue of a new journal, *Teaching Theology and Religion.*[20] While acknowledging the diversity that is to be valued in the distinction between theology and religious studies, he believes that there is no justification for dividing the field between them, especially if it is assumed that they cannot coexist in the same institution. At their best, the fields overlap extensively and reinforce each other. We need to find a better paradigm for organizing our work, one that accords with actual practices and not with an arbitrary division. Ford proposes a general overarching definition: "Theological and religious studies deals with questions of meaning, truth, beauty, and practice raised in relation to religions and pursued through a range of academic disciplines." This "ecology" of the field is articulated by Ford in terms of four dimensions to which both religious and theological studies should attend: the fascinating, inexhaustible phenomena of religion; the extraordinary ethical demands raised by questions of truth and goodness; the inexorable particularities of the subject matter combined with the recognition that the major religious traditions "have an equally inexorable thrust towards universality, and towards trust in a Wisdom that can make the deepest sense of all reality"; and finally a recognition that theology and religious studies are "divinely involving," having to do with God or analogues of God, aiming (in David Kelsey's words[21]) "to understand God truly." Ford believes that different programs and institutions will emphasize one or another of these dimensions but that they should all be present whenever religion is studied. This is a better way of articulating the distinctiveness of particular programs than in terms of the stereotypical distinction between "theology" and "religious studies." I believe Ford's analysis and proposals make a very important contribution.

One difficult aspect of our question concerns the way in which the various disciplines or specialty fields comprising religious and theological studies might be brought together to form a coherent program. I have been involved for several years in discussing this matter at the graduate level, both in my own institution and through a consultation on the doctoral education of theological faculties sponsored by the Auburn Center for the Study of Theological Education.[22] I have concluded that curricular reform and programmatic restructuring is best accomplished by letting it seep up from below rather than by imposing it from above. Individuals can create impressive organizing schemes about which it is very difficult to obtain consensus from a faculty. I am convinced by Charles Anderson's insight that access to wisdom comes *through* the academic disciplines, not around them or apart from them. Considering the vastness of knowledge, the disciplines are here to stay, and while they are constantly redefining their frontiers and methods they continue to be the principal means by which knowledge is organized in the university. Our task is to bring the subdisciplines of religion/theology together in a collaborative endeavor, to make them more porous and interactive, to persuade them to share in meta-field thinking about what constitutes religious and theological studies, to invite them to think together about both religious differences and the common good, and to encourage among them interdisciplinary and cross-cultural studies. How this works itself out in specific programs of study will vary greatly. Perhaps it can be agreed that we want doctoral students to acquire both breadth and depth of knowledge, to have both refined critical skills and passion for the subject matter, and to demonstrate both competence as a research scholar and gifts as a teacher. In the final analysis, it does not matter very much whether students are preparing to teach in a religious studies department or a theological seminary, for the qualities of paideia in these settings are more similar than they are different, and the contingencies of the job market are such that doctoral students cannot really anticipate the conditions in which they will find themselves.

Another difficult aspect of the question about the place of paideia in religious and theological studies concerns the purpose and structure of the theological school or seminary. Here the focus is on the education of leadership for churches, synagogues, and other religious institutions as opposed to the preparation of teachers and scholars of religion/theology. David Kelsey[23] points to a potential conflict between the intrinsic purpose of a theological school, which he says is "to seek to understand God more truly," and its principal rationale for existing, namely, to train leadership for an indispensable social practice. Leadership training in most cases is what unifies the theological curriculum, which is at once scientific and professional, and it is not easily compatible with the contemplative moment of paideia. Moreover, God cannot be understood directly but only by focusing study on various subject matters (scripture, tradition, liturgy, ethics, theology, religious experience, pastoral care, and so forth), not as ends in themselves but as they bear on actual worshiping communities of faith.[24] Here guild interests overpower the desire to understand God truly, but they cannot be short-circuited in a homogenized spirituality. The overarching goal of a theological school sides with the "Athens" ideal of paideia, while the range of things studied and the critical thinking employed are appropriated from the "Berlin" model of science (*Wissenschaft*). Thus Kelsey arrives at what he calls the *theological school paradox:* "It is precisely by being schooled in a way that is governed by an apparently nonutilitarian . . . overarching goal (that is, to understand God simply for the sake of understanding God) that persons can best be prepared to provide church leadership." This is because church leaders are not in the strict sense "professionals" and do not rely on technical rationality but on a "wisdom rooted in faith, hope, and love of God."[25] Kelsey's proposal is guided by H. Richard Niebuhr's insight that the passionate desire to love God intellectually requires disinterested inquiry, and that the latter must be guided by the former to displace love of self.[26]

I think that the theological school paradox is also the paradox of religious and theological studies and of liberal education in general. It is by being schooled in a way that is governed by the overarching goal of paideia—the nurturing and enhancement of a wisdom oriented to human flourishing, which in its highest expression entails understanding God, the ultimate mystery, for its own sake—that persons are best prepared to assume the responsibilities of citizenship and to lead discerning lives in their chosen professions. The overarching goal incorporates all the discipline and rigor that science can muster, but it prevents science from becoming an end in itself; it reorients it from self-centeredness to reality-centeredness, from intellectual hubris to the love of God and neighbor. The theological proviso specifies that the wisdom acquired through the formative journey of life is ultimately the gift of God's Wisdom, the manifestation of God's pedagogical presence in the world. We are reminded of Irenaeus's axiom, "the glory of God is human beings made fully alive," to which he immediately adds, "the aliveness of human beings is in beholding God" (*gloria Dei vivens homo, vita autem hominus visio Dei*).[27] Theologically speaking, it is for the sake of God and the glory of God that we do all that we do. This theological proviso certainly cannot be assumed to be an axiom of liberal education. Yet God is glorified and beheld not directly but by making human beings fully alive. That is a task in which theology and education can share.

The conclusions offered by this chapter seem rather modest. I do not have a magic bullet with which to solve the complex problems facing liberal education in general and religious and theological studies in particular. I do not offer many concrete proposals of my own for defining the purpose of the university, integrating the disciplines, resolving the dispute between religious and theological studies, or restructuring theological education. Others have thought about these problems longer and more creatively than I, and I incorporate some of their ideas.

I have attempted to provide a larger perspective in which to reflect on these issues. My basic conviction is that a religious dimension pervades all of education whether it is recognized or not. If it is recognized, everything is cast into a different light, provided with a perspective by which finite goods and goals are both legitimated and de-absolutized. In this perspective, disciplinary differences do not seem so important, and the kind of human transformation that education seeks to bring about is a shared responsibility of everyone involved. This perspective is a contribution that a theology of education can make to the educational enterprise as a whole. Obviously I do not claim that one must have a theological conviction in order to engage in transformative pedagogy. But genuine, radical transformation requires a power that transcends any teacher or program. The best teachers seem to be aware of the mysterious presence of this power in what they are doing, and toward it they assume an attitude of reference. With bell hooks, they believe that there is an aspect of their vocation that is sacred. Open discussion of this matter would contribute to liberal education.

I tried to show how Christian theologians incorporated the Hellenic ideal of paideia, radicalizing it through their understanding of sin and redemption (as opposed to ignorance and recollection), but without weakening the Greek eros for knowledge as a whole by creating a parochial zone of saving knowledge. They recognized but one truth and one paideia, complex, multifaceted, and inexhaustible, to be sure, but not divisible into sacred and profane realms. This has implications for the integration of secular and religious studies today. I suggested that the various elements of a postmodern transformative pedagogy—education and life formation, the rhythm of education, constructive and interactive knowledge, education as the practice of freedom, and connected teaching and cooperative learning—all point to a religious depth dimension of the pedagogical process. Thus no responsible liberal education can exclude attention to religion. I attempted to unpack the rhythm of education by suggesting that it encompasses three interrelated moments: critical thinking, heightened imagination, and liberating practice. God's Wisdom, I suggested, drives thinking to its depths, raises imagination to its heights, and draws practice to its telos. These moments come together in a *critical engagement* with subject matter, and from this perspective the differing emphases of religious and theological studies are not as important as their common pedagogy. Finally, I argued that education actually occurs through the interaction of outwardly mediated resources and an inner ingestion or appropriation of what has been given: it is a mediated immediacy, entailing both revelation and inspiration, history and spirit, culture and psyche. The teacher facilitates this mediation but does not control it.

These proposals are all primarily formal. The material content of God's Wisdom will differ in accord with the determinate religious traditions through which it appears. *Christian* theology of education takes its orientation on the paradigmatic figure of Jesus of Nazareth, who incarnates God's Wisdom in his teaching and practice, his way of living and dying. The central image of his teaching was that of a new and radically open community of freedom in which God's Wisdom prevails as opposed to the foolishness and weakness of human wisdom. This divine Wisdom overthrows the dominant logic of the world (hierarchical, authoritarian, juridical, dualistic) in favor of a new logic, that of grace, love, and freedom, of uncoerced and fully reciprocal communicative practices. Jesus taught not in the form of propositions and laws but by means of engaging people in conversation and forcing them to reflect on the deeper meaning of their convictions. He made use of metaphors and parables to depict a new reality that could not be described directly. His teaching continues to work salvifically, not in a magical way, but by providing resources through which, again and again, human beings can break the grip of the dominant paradigms, battle against illusion and fear, find purpose in life, be pulled out of preoccupation with self into an unrequited love for others, and participate in the open-ended, never-finished project of building a new world, God's project. This is a model of teaching and a vision of human flourishing that seems as relevant to the complex problems facing education today as it was in a far different time and culture.

NOTES

The epigraph is from a letter of George Eliot (Mary Ann Evans) to Sara Sophia Hennell, 27 November 1847. *The George Eliot Letters*, 9 vols., ed. Gordon S. Haight (New Haven, Conn.: Yale University Press, 1954–56, 1978), 1:242.

1. Introduction: Teaching as a Religious Vocation

1. Alfred North Whitehead, *The Aims of Education and Other Essays* (1929; New York: Free Press, 1967), 14. The philosopher of education Robert Ulich argues similarly that liberal education is "fundamentally religious." See his essay "The Meaning of Liberal Education," in Christian Gauss, ed., *The Teaching of Religion in American Higher Education* (New York: Ronald Press Co., 1951), chap. 2, esp. 56–61.
2. Martin Buber, "Education" (1926), in *Between Man and Man,* trans. Ronald Gregor Smith (Boston: Beacon Press, 1955), esp. 102–3.
3. Buber, "The Education of Character" (1939), in *Between Man and Man,* 116–17.
4. Bernard Eugene Meland, *Higher Education and the Human Spirit* (Chicago: University of Chicago Press, 1953), chaps. 1–2.
5. bell hooks, *Teaching to Transgress: Education as the Practice of Freedom* (New York: Routledge, 1994), 13.
6. Ibid., 206.
7. John Dewey, *Democracy and Education: An Introduction to the Philosophy of Education* (1916; New York: Free Press, 1966), chap. 1.
8. William G. Perry, Jr., *Forms of Intellectual and Ethical Development in the College Years* (New York: Holt, Rinehart & Winston, 1970), chaps. 1, 5; pp. 34–35, 134–37.
9. See Thomas Armstrong's description of it in *Multiple Intelligences in the Classroom* (Alexandria, Va.: Association for Supervision and Curriculum Development, 1994), 3, 6–8.
10. Ibid., 4–6.
11. A similar idea is already found in the eighteenth-century philosopher J. G. Herder (see below, p. 41).
12. See Peter C. Hodgson, *Winds of the Spirit: A Constructive Christian*

Theology (Louisville, Ky.: Westminster John Knox Press, 1994), 258.

13. Werner Jaeger, *Early Christianity and Greek Paideia* (Cambridge, Mass.: Harvard University Press, 1961), 86.

14. Horace Bushnell, *Christian Nurture* (1861; New York: Charles Scribner's Sons, 1886), 9, 65.

15. Edward Farley, *The Fragility of Knowledge: Theological Education in the Church and University* (Philadelphia: Fortress Press, 1988), 180. See chaps. 4, 7, 8.

2. God as Teacher: Classical and Modern Theologies

1. Stephen F. Bayne, Jr., "God Is the Teacher," in *The Christian Idea of Education*, ed. Edmund Fuller (New Haven, Conn.: Yale University Press, 1957), 255–56.

2. Amy Plantinga Pauw, in a panel sponsored by the *Journal of Teaching Theology and Religion* on "The Meaning and Ends of Teaching Religion," American Academy of Religion, November 22, 1997.

3. Gabriel Moran, *Showing How: The Act of Teaching* (Valley Forge, Pa.: Trinity Press International, 1997), 43, 47.

4. Frank Crüsemann, *The Torah: Theology and Social History of Old Testament Law*, trans. Allan W. Mahnke (Minneapolis: Fortress Press, 1996), 1–2.

5. Jacob Neusner, "Knowing God in the Torah," in Jacob Neusner and Bruce D. Chilton, *Revelation: The Torah and the Bible* (Valley Forge, Pa.: Trinity Press International, 1995), 25, 30.

6. Ibid., 31–36, 38–40, 45, 49.

7. Elliot R. Wolfson, *Through a Speculum That Shines: Vision and Imagination in Medieval Jewish Mysticism* (Princeton, N.J.: Princeton University Press, 1994), 376, quoting *Zohar* 2:60a.

8. Ibid., 26, 147–48, 214, 305, 344, 353–56. Surprisingly, this idea is also picked up by John Calvin (see below, n. 52).

9. Israel M. Goldman, *Lifelong Learning among Jews: Adult Education in Judaism from Biblical Times to the Twentieth Century* (New York: KTAV Publishing House, 1975), 63 (quoting Rabbi Joshua ben Karha). Cf. Crüsemann, *The Torah*, 5, 365.

10. Wolfson, *Through a Speculum That Shines*, 375–76.

11. Wolfson writes: "The symbolic vision bridges the gap between the invisible and the visible, the spiritual and the corporeal, by lending approximate expression to the transcendental truth." Ibid., 66. He discusses in detail the matter of the visualization of God; see the whole of chap. 1, "Israel: The One Who Sees God," esp. p. 51.

12. See Goldman, *Lifelong Learning among Jews,* 27, 43; Neusner, "Knowing God in the Torah," 40–41, 46–47.

13. Goldman, *Lifelong Learning among Jews,* 1–2, 4–7, 49–50.

14. Ibid., chaps. 2–4 and pp. 305–7.

15. Neusner, "Knowing God in the Torah," 50–51, 72–79, 99–103.

16. Werner Jaeger, *Paideia: The Ideals of Greek Culture,* trans. Gilbert Highet, 3 vols. (New York: Oxford University Press, 1943), vol. 2, p. 18; see pp. 13–26. Mastery of the Socratic ideas and the Platonic literature is a major intellectual undertaking. I do not claim to have accomplished it myself; instead I rely principally on Jaeger's magisterial study.

17. G. W. F. Hegel, *Vorlesungen über die Geschichte der Philosophie,* ed. Pierre Garniron and Walter Jaeschke, part 2 (*Vorlesungen: Ausgewählte Nachschriften und Manuskripte,* vol. 7; Hamburg: Felix Meiner Verlag, 1989), 139–44.

18. Jaeger, *Paideia,* vol. 2, pp. 27–32, 37–39, 41–46, 59–70.

19. Martha C. Nussbaum, *Cultivating Humanity: A Classical Defense of Reform in Liberal Education* (Cambridge, Mass.: Harvard University Press, 1997), 1–46, 293–330; quotation from p. 26.

20. Jaeger, *Paideia,* vol. 2, pp. 84–86.

21. Ibid., vol. 2, chaps. 4–7. See Hegel, *Vorlesungen über die Geschichte der Philosophie,* part 3 (*Vorlesungen,* vol. 8, 1996), 19–36.

22. Jaeger, *Paideia,* vol. 2, chap. 8; also pp. 228–30.

23. For what follows on *The Republic,* see Jaeger, *Paideia,* vol. 2, chap. 9, esp. pp. 217–19, 286–87, 291–300.

24. Ibid., vol. 3, chap. 10, esp. pp. 241–43. In the *Timaeus* the picture is not that of a fixed hierarchical structure of forms but of a flow in which the demiurge constantly struggles to in-form ever-resistant matter. This shows the fluidity of Plato's thinking about the divine.

25. Ibid., vol. 3, pp. 244–45, 261–62.

26. Werner Jaeger, *Early Christianity and Greek Paideia* (Cambridge, Mass.: Harvard University Press, 1961), 12.

27. Ibid., 12–26.

28. Ibid., 47.

29. Ibid., 60–62.

30. For the following summary, see Clement of Alexandria, *The Instructor (Paedagogus),* in *The Ante-Nicene Fathers,* vol. 2 (Grand Rapids: Wm. B. Eerdmans Publishing Co., 1962), 209–37.

31. Jaeger, *Early Christianity and Greek Paideia,* 65–67.

32. See Origen, *De principiis,* in *The Ante-Nicene Fathers,* vol. 4 (Grand Rapids: Wm. B. Eerdmans Publishing Co., 1956), 239–384.

33. J. N. D. Kelly, *Early Christian Doctrines* (London: Adam & Charles Black, 1958), 261–63.

34. This work remains untranslated, and I rely on Werner Jaeger's interpretation of it in *Early Christianity and Greek Paideia*, 86–100; and in *Two Rediscovered Works of Ancient Christian Literature: Gregory of Nyssa and Macarius* (Leiden: E. J. Brill, 1954), 73–113.

35. Jaeger, *Early Christianity and Greek Paideia*, 87.

36. Jaeger, *Early Christianity and Greek Paideia*, 88; *Two Rediscovered Works*, 92–96, 103–6.

37. Jaeger, *Early Christianity and Greek Paideia*, 93–98.

38. Augustine, *The Confessions*, in *Basic Writings of Saint Augustine*, vol. 1, ed. Whitney J. Oates (New York: Random House, 1948); see esp. 10–19.

39. See Augustine, *Basic Writings*, vol. 1, pp. 361–95. A recent edition of this text is found in Augustine, *Against the Academicians and The Teacher*, trans. with introduction and notes by Peter King (Indianapolis: Hackett Publishing Co., 1995).

40. Thomas Aquinas, *Truth* (*De veritate*), trans. James V. McGlynn, vol. 2 (Chicago: Henry Regnery Co., 1953).

41. Ibid., 82–86.

42. Ibid., 90, 98–101.

43. Bonaventure, *The Journey of the Mind to God*, trans. Philotheus Boehner, ed. Stephen F. Brown (Indianapolis: Hackett Publishing Co., 1993).

44. Ibid., 38–39. See Pseudo-Dionysius, *On Mystical Theology*, 1.1.

45. See Dennis E. Tamburello, *Union with Christ: John Calvin and the Mysticism of St. Bernard* (Louisville, Ky.: Westminster John Knox Press, 1994), chap. 1.

46. See Serene Jones, *Calvin and the Rhetoric of Piety* (Louisville, Ky.: Westminster John Knox Press, 1995), esp. chaps. 1 and 6.

47. Ibid., 197.

48. Ibid., 187–92, 198–202.

49. John Calvin, *Institutes of the Christian Religion*, ed. John T. McNeill, trans. Ford Lewis Battles, 2 vols. (Philadelphia: Westminster Press, 1960). I quote at length from this text because Calvin's language is so rich, nuanced, and suggestive. It is difficult to separate the substance of what is said from the precise way that it is being said. The *Institutes* are a rhetorical tour de force.

50. See n. 9 to *Inst.* 3.1.4; also 4.14.9.

51. Calvin says that only the latter two are regularly constituted offices since the church can never do without them, whereas the first three were needed at the beginning and now from time to time as occasions demand (*Inst.* 4.3.4).

52. See the references above (nn. 7, 8) to Wolfson's *Through a Speculum That Shines*. All this is found in *Inst.* 4.1.5.

53. My focus of attention on Calvin is partly explained by my own association with the Reformed tradition. Martin Luther also wrote on education, primarily in some rather obscure works on the education of children that have not proved helpful for my purposes.

54. Horace Bushnell, *Christian Nurture* (New York: Charles Scribner's Sons, 1886). The most recent edition was published by Pilgrim Press in 1994. Bushnell was acutely aware of the figurative character of theological language, and his writing is filled with fascinating metaphors and expressions. I have attempted to capture some of them in quotations.

55. Ibid., 9–10.

56. Ibid., 15–17, 21.

57. Ibid., 12–13, 22, 26–28, 31–32. This is a very important point for Bushnell. He elaborates on it in chap. 4, "The Organic Unity of the Family." There he writes: "A power is exerted by parents over children, not only when they teach, encourage, persuade, and govern, but without any purposed control whatever. The bond is so intimate that they do it unconsciously and undesignedly—they must do it" (p. 93).

58. Ibid., 17–18, 49–51, 57.

59. Ibid., 33–40, 59.

60. Ibid., 65–70, 23.

61. Horace Bushnell, *Sermons*, ed. Conrad Cherry (New York: Paulist Press, 1985), 37–54. The treatise was begun in 1875, a year before he died.

62. *Lessing's Theological Writings,* ed. and trans. Henry Chadwick (Stanford, Calif.: Stanford University Press, 1957), 82–98.

63. As suggested by Henry Chadwick in his introduction to *Lessing's Theological Writings,* esp. 43–48.

64. I am guided here by the interpretation of Toshimasa Yasukata in *Lessing and the German Enlightenment: A Study of Lessing's Philosophy of Religion* (Tokyo: Subunsha Publishing Co., 1998); forthcoming in English.

65. Selections are translated in Johann Gottfried Herder, *Against Pure Reason: Writings on Religion, Language, and History*, trans. and ed. Marcia Bunge (Minneapolis: Fortress Press, 1993), 38–48.

66. See the introduction by Bunge, 12–19.

67. Excerpts in *Against Pure Reason,* 48–58. The entire work was translated by T. O. Churchill in 1800. An abridgement of this translation, edited by Frank E. Manuel, was published by the University of Chicago Press in 1968.

68. These passages are all found in the excerpt translated by Bunge, esp. 49–57. On George Eliot, see below, chap. 4, n. 54.

69. During the Enlightenment there began to appear philosophies and theories of education that were no longer specifically religious in content, although theological ideas resided in the background of many of them. Thinking about education was becoming secular, a process that already had begun in preceding centuries with the works of Erasmus, Francis Bacon, John Comenius, and John Locke. Among the great eighteenth-century theorists were Friedrich Froebel, Johann Heinrich Pestalozzi, Jean Jacques Rousseau, and Friedrich Schiller. To consider all of these figures would take us too far afield. Another figure I have chosen not to discuss is Immanuel Kant, whose lectures on pedagogy, which were closely connected with his philosophy of history, were influenced by Lessing and Herder. In these lectures Kant distinguishes between three stages: nurture (the child cared for and fed as purely a part of nature), discipline (the training of mind and body under the rule of prudence), and cultivation (*Bildung*, moral education, including discovery of the moral law within). See Lewis Beck, "Kant on Education," in *Education in the Eighteenth Century*, ed. John D. Browning (New York: Garland Publishing Co., 1979), 10–24. Kant's philosophy in general was, of course, a major influence on Hegel. Finally there occurred in Germany in the late eighteenth and early nineteenth centuries a lively debate about university education among Kant, Friedrich Schelling, Johann Gottlieb Fichte, and Friedrich Schleiermacher, to which I have not attended either. Schleiermacher lectured extensively on pedagogy, but these lectures do not seem germane to my project, and I can find little in his major work, *The Christian Faith*, that bears on a theology of education. Thus I pass over all of these figures and turn directly to Hegel.

70. See *Lectures on the Philosophy of Religion*, one-volume edition, *The Lectures of 1827*, ed. and trans. Peter C. Hodgson et al. (Berkeley and Los Angeles: University of California Press, 1988), 122, 173n–174n, 422.

71. "Religion Is One of Our Greatest Concerns in Life," in *G. W. F. Hegel: Theologian of the Spirit*, ed. Peter C. Hodgson (Minneapolis: Fortress Press, 1997), 39–57.

72. See *Phänomenologie des Geistes*, ed. Johannes Hoffmeister (Hamburg: Felix Meiner Verlag, 1952), 26–27. This passage is translated in *Hegel: Theologian of the Spirit*, 98–99. In the translation by J. B. Baillie (2d ed. rev.; London: George Allen & Unwin, 1949), it is found on pp. 89–90.

73. See Robert R. Williams, "Reason, Authority, and Recognition in Hegel's Theory of Education," paper presented at the World Congress of Philosophy, August 1998. I am guided by Williams's in-

terpretation at a number of points. Hegel's 1817–18 Heidelberg lectures on the philosophy of right were published in German in 1983 and have appeared in English as *Lectures on Natural Right and Political Science,* trans. J. Michael Stewart and Peter C. Hodgson (Berkeley and Los Angeles: University of California Press, 1995). Hegel himself published these lectures as a textbook in 1820; the latest English translation is *Elements of the Philosophy of Right,* ed. Allen W. Wood, trans. H. B. Nisbet (Cambridge: Cambridge University Press, 1991). I cite both versions below, abbreviated respectively as *NRPS* and *PR.*

74. *PR* § 151.
75. *NRPS* §§ 85–86, *PR* §§ 174–75.
76. *NRPS* § 86, *PR* § 153.
77. *PR* § 187.
78. *NRPS* § 158.
79. *PR* § 187.
80. *Lectures on the Philosophy of Religion,* 155–61, esp. 160–61.
81. Søren Kierkegaard, *Philosophical Fragments,* ed. and trans. Howard V. Hong and Edna H. Hong (Princeton, N.J.: Princeton University Press, 1985), chaps. 1–2 (pp. 9–36). The "thought-project" of the *Fragments* (chap. 1) is to think "God as Teacher and Savior" (chap. 2), which entails "the absolute paradox" (chap. 3 with its "appendix") and raises questions about historical knowledge and the meaning of contemporaneity (chaps. 4, 5 and the "interlude" between them).
82. Ibid., 21.
83. Ibid., 32–33.
84. My thoughts in these final paragraphs are stimulated by some challenging questions put to me by Edward Farley on the basis of his reading an earlier draft.

3. Transformative Pedagogy: Modern and Postmodern Theories

1. These include writings by Martin Buber, Bernard Meland, Denise Carmody, Maria Harris, Mary Elizabeth Mullino Moore, Gabriel Moran, and Parker Palmer. In addition, works by Edward Farley, David Kelsey, Rebecca Chopp, and others on theological education make a very important contribution. These will all be considered below. An exception that I shall not be considering is that of John Henry Newman's *The Idea of a University* (1873). This is not precisely a theological work, although it is written from a broadly theological perspective. Newman's basic convictions about the cultivation of intellect and the underlying, unifying goals of

university education have been more effectively articulated, in my judgment, by some of the recent literature to which I shall refer, but without the problematic aspects of his thought. As David Kelsey suggests, Newman's social assumptions, view of human rationality, and vision of fulfilled human life are all deeply troubling, reflecting as they do the social and intellectual elite of late nineteenth-century Britain. See David H. Kelsey, *Between Athens and Berlin: The Theological Education Debate* (Grand Rapids: Wm. B. Eerdmans Publishing Co., 1993), chap. 2.

2. For an excellent analysis of various types of postmodernity, see Paul Lakeland, *Postmodernity: Christian Identity in a Fragmented Age* (Minneapolis: Fortress Press, 1997), chap. 1.

3. John Dewey, *Democracy and Education: An Introduction to the Philosophy of Education* (1916; New York: Free Press, 1966), chap. 1.

4. Ibid., 2–3.

5. Gabriel Moran argues that the verb "to teach" means "to show" (from an Anglo-Saxon root meaning "sign," "symbol")—to show someone how to do something. What teaching and education ultimately show us is "how to live and how to die." *Showing How: The Act of Teaching* (Valley Forge, Pa.: Trinity Press International, 1997), 37–39.

6. Dewey, *Democracy and Education*, 3–7; Paul Tillich, *Theology of Culture*, ed. Robert C. Kimball (New York: Oxford University Press, 1959), 42.

7. Dewey, *Democracy and Education*, 11–15. See, for example, Martin Heidegger's analysis of "being-in-the-world" in *Being and Time*, trans. Joan Stambaugh (Albany, N.Y.: State University of New York Press, 1996), 49ff.

8. Charles W. Anderson, *Prescribing the Life of the Mind: An Essay on the Purpose of the University, the Aims of Liberal Education, the Competence of Citizens, and the Cultivation of Practical Reason* (Madison, Wis.: University of Wisconsin Press, 1993).

9. Ibid., 44–58.

10. Ibid., 90–92.

11. Dewey, *Democracy and Education*, 49–51.

12. Bernard Eugene Meland, *Higher Education and the Human Spirit* (Chicago: University of Chicago Press, 1953), chap. 1, esp. 2, 5–6. See also Martin Buber's essays on "Education" and "The Education of Character" in *Between Man and Man*, trans. Ronald Gregor Smith (Boston: Beacon Press, 1955).

13. Thomas Armstrong, *Multiple Intelligences in the Classroom* (Alexandria, Va.: Association for Supervision and Curriculum Development, 1994), pp. x, 1–3, 49.

14. Moran, *Showing How*, chap. 7.

15. Edward Farley, *The Fragility of Knowledge: Theological Education in the Church and the University* (Philadelphia: Fortress Press, 1988), chap. 5 ("Can Church Education Be Theological Education?").

16. See Kelsey, *Between Athens and Berlin: The Theological Education Debate*. I shall return to Kelsey's provocative study of this matter in chaps. 4 and 5.

17. See Werner Jaeger, *Paideia: The Ideals of Greek Culture*, trans. Gilbert Highet, vol. 2 (New York: Oxford University Press, 1943), 313–19.

18. Hegel himself did not use the language of thesis, antithesis, and synthesis with which he is popularly associated. The problem with this expression is its suggestion that the antithesis is simply the logical opposite of the thesis, an opposing thesis. But for Hegel there is a crucial logical difference between the first term, that of universality, and the second, particularity, which is not another universal. Nor is individuality a mechanical synthesis of the first two terms. Rather, it represents a dialectical advance into subjectivity. See *Science of Logic*, trans. A. V. Miller (London: George Allen & Unwin, 1969), 664–704.

19. Alfred North Whitehead, *The Aims of Education and Other Essays* (New York: Free Press, 1967), chap. 2. The essay on "The Rhythm of Education" was first published in 1922.

20. Ibid., chap. 3; quotation from p. 29.

21. Ibid., 30–31.

22. Ibid., 31–39, 94–95.

23. Mary Elizabeth Mullino Moore, *Teaching from the Heart: Theology and Educational Method* (Minneapolis: Fortress Press, 1991), chap. 3, esp. pp. 79–84.

24. William G. Perry, Jr., *Forms of Intellectual and Ethical Development in the College Years: A Scheme* (New York: Holt, Rinehart & Winston, 1968, 1970), esp. chaps. 1, 5, 6.

25. I take these terms to mean essentially the same thing with slightly different nuances. "Constructive" emphasizes the creative role of imagination in bringing things together into a meaningful coherence, while "constructed" emphasizes that the objects of knowledge are, in the form we know them, human products. See my discussion of "construction in a deconstructive age" in *Winds of the Spirit: A Constructive Christian Theology* (Louisville, Ky.: Westminster John Knox Press, 1994), 37–41.

26. Mary Field Belenky, Blythe McVicker Clincy, Nancy Rule Goldberger, and Jill Mattuck Tarule, *Women's Ways of Knowing: The Development of Self, Voice, and Mind* (New York: Basic Books, 1986).

27. Ibid., 9–15.

28. Ibid., 133, 137.

29. Ibid., 138–140.

30. Ibid., 140–41. The authors quote scientist-philosopher Michael Polanyi to this effect in his description of "personal knowledge." See *Personal Knowledge: Towards a Post-Critical Philosophy* (Chicago: University of Chicago Press, 1958), chap. 6.

31. *Women's Ways of Knowing*, 142–150.

32. Meland, *Higher Education and the Human Spirit*, 22–25.

33. Ibid., 26–29.

34. See John C. Bean, *Engaging Ideas: The Professor's Guide to Integrating Writing, Critical Thinking, and Active Learning in the Classroom* (San Francisco: Jossey-Bass, 1996), chap. 1; and Linda B. Nilson, *Teaching at Its Best: A Research-Based Resource for the Vanderbilt Teaching Community* (Center for Teaching, Vanderbilt University, 1995; forthcoming from Anker Publishing Co.), chaps. 10–11, 15.

35. J. G. Herder, *Ideen zur Philosophie der Geschichte der Menschheit*, in *Sprachphilosophische Schriften*, ed. Erich Heintel, 2d ed. (Hamburg: Felix Meiner Verlag, 1964), 164. For his association of liberation with language, see 19–30.

36. G. W. F. Hegel, *Lectures on the Philosophy of World History. Introduction: Reason in History*, trans. H. B. Nisbet with an introduction by Duncan Forbes (Cambridge: Cambridge University Press, 1975), 35–55. See my discussion of Hegel's philosophy of history in *God in History: Shapes of Freedom* (Nashville: Abingdon Press, 1989), 115–130. It is obvious that Hegel had not yet arrived at a truly global consciousness, although the logic of his position points beyond Eurocentrism.

37. G. W. F. Hegel, *Lectures on Natural Right and Political Science*, ed. Staff of the Hegel Archives, trans. J. Michael Stewart and Peter C. Hodgson (Berkeley and Los Angeles: University of California Press, 1995), § 85.

38. G. W. F. Hegel, *Elements of the Philosophy of Right*, ed. Allen W. Wood, trans. H. B. Nisbet (Cambridge: Cambridge University Press, 1991), § 4. See Hodgson, *God in History*, 219.

39. In her book, *Teaching to Transgress: Education as the Practice of Freedom* (New York: Routledge, 1994); bell hooks is the pen name of Gloria Watkins, a distinguished African American teacher of English literature.

40. Ibid., 13. For what follows, see chap. 1.

41. Ibid., 15–21.

42. Ibid., 202–7.

43. Paulo Freire, *Pedagogy of the Oppressed*, trans. Myra Bergman

Ramos (New York: Herder & Herder, 1972). See also his *Education for Critical Consciousness* (New York: Seabury Press, 1973).

44. *Pedagogy of the Oppressed*, chap. 1. See esp. pp. 19–20, 32–33, 52–54.
45. Ibid., 66–67; see the whole of chap. 2.
46. Ibid., 69, 71.
47. bell hooks, *Teaching to Transgress*, chap. 2, esp. pp. 26–27. The quotation is from King's *Where Do We Go from Here: Chaos or Community?* (New York: Harper & Row, 1967).
48. Ibid., 28.
49. Henry A. Giroux, *Border Crossings: Cultural Workers and the Politics of Education* (New York: Routledge, 1992), chap. 1.
50. Dewey, *Democracy and Education*, chap. 7, esp. p. 87.
51. From the introduction to their edited book, *Between Borders: Pedagogy and the Politics of Cultural Studies* (New York: Routledge, 1993). See also *Multicultural Education, Critical Pedagogy, and the Politics of Difference*, ed. Christine E. Sleeter and Peter L. McLaren (Albany, N.Y.: State University of New York Press, 1995), especially the introductory essay.
52. bell hooks, *Teaching to Transgress*, 129; see chap. 10.
53. Moacir Gadotti, *Pedagogy of Praxis: A Dialectical Philosophy of Education*, trans. John Milton (Albany, N.Y.: State University of New York Press, 1996), pp. ix–xvii (from an interview with Peter McLaren).
54. Giroux, *Border Crossings*, 165.
55. Gerald Graff, *Beyond the Culture Wars: How Teaching the Conflicts Can Revitalize American Education* (New York: W. W. Norton & Co., 1992), 12–15.
56. Giroux, *Border Crossings*, 20.
57. Ibid., 19–21.
58. Ibid., 23–26, 28–30, 32, 35, 89–95, 166, 174.
59. Belenky et al., *Women's Ways of Knowing*, 194–96.
60. Ibid., 217–219.
61. Ibid., 214–17, 228.
62. Ibid., 225–27.
63. Buber, *Between Man and Man*, 91–101.
64. bell hooks discusses this in a helpful way in *Teaching to Transgress*, 134–59, 191–98.
65. Another approach to connected teaching is through the spiritual traditions. See Parker J. Palmer, *To Know as We Are Known: Education as a Spiritual Journey* (San Francisco: HarperCollins, 1993). The pain that permeates education is "the pain of disconnection," writes Palmer, and he believes that spirituality can help us acquire a passion for connection and wholeness. Knowing is a form

of loving whose goal is the reunification of broken selves and the world. The task of teaching is to create a space in which obedience to truth and the community of truth is practiced. Such practice depends on a teacher who has a living relationship with the subject and who invites students into that relationship as full partners. Parker envisions this relationship as one of friendship. See esp. the preface and chaps. 1, 5, 6.

66. Moran, *Showing How*, 40–42, 51–57, 59–79. The guru-disciple relationship found in some forms of Hinduism and Buddhism is especially illuminating, suggests Moran: the disciple strives to imitate and identify with the guru, while the guru asks nothing of the student and knows that he is not really the teacher at all. Apart from my discussion in the next chapter of the guru as christological model, I am not acquainted with Asian theories and practices of education. This potentially very fruitful resource is almost totally absent from the recent pedagogical literature.

67. Nilson, *Teaching at Its Best*, chap. 15, esp. 95–98; Bean, *Engaging Ideas*, chaps. 9–10.

68. Graff, *Beyond the Culture Wars*, chap. 9.

69. See Palmer, *To Know as We Are Known*, chaps. 2 ("Education as Spiritual Formation") and 7 ("The Spiritual Formation of Teachers").

4. God's Wisdom: Education as Paideia

1. Maria Harris discusses the etymology of "wisdom" and identifies "four wisdoms": foolishness (the element of imagination and play), creativity, wholeness, and worship. See *Teaching and Religious Imagination: An Essay in the Theology of Teaching* (San Francisco: Harper & Row, 1987), 152–55. See also the *Oxford English Dictionary*, 2d ed. (Oxford: Clarendon Press, 1989).

2. Edward Farley, *The Fragility of Knowledge: Theological Education in the Church and the University* (Philadelphia: Fortress Press, 1988), 87–88, 118.

3. John B. Cobb, Jr., "Theology against the Disciplines," in *Shifting Boundaries: Contextual Approaches to the Structure of Theological Education*, ed. Barbara G. Wheeler and Edward Farley (Louisville, Ky.: Westminster/John Knox Press, 1991), 248.

4. David H. Kelsey, *To Understand God Truly: What's Theological about a Theological School* (Louisville, Ky.: Westminster/John Knox Press, 1992), 34.

5. Elizabeth A. Johnson, *She Who Is: The Mystery of God in Feminist Theological Discourse* (New York: Crossroad, 1992), 86–90 (quotation from p. 87). Johnson is drawing here on a large body of bib-

lical scholarship, notably works by Elisabeth Schüssler Fiorenza, Ulrich Wilckens, R. B. Scott, Roland Murphy, Gerhard von Rad, Bernhard Lang, R. N. Whybray, and Helmut Ringgren.

6. Ibid., 91.

7. Elisabeth Schüssler Fiorenza, *Jesus: Miriam's Child, Sophia's Prophet: Critical Issues in Feminist Christology* (New York: Continuum Publishing Co., 1994), 133–36.

8. For the above I am indebted to Denis Edwards, *Jesus the Wisdom of God: An Ecological Theology* (Maryknoll, N.Y.: Orbis Books, 1995), 19–33.

9. Johnson, *She Who Is*, 82–86, 94.

10. See J. N. D. Kelly, *Early Christian Doctrines* (London: Adam & Charles Black, 1958), 104, 106.

11. See Peter C. Hodgson, *Winds of the Spirit: A Constructive Christian Theology* (Louisville, Ky.: Westminster John Knox Press, 1994), chap. 17.

12. See *Winds of the Spirit*, chap. 11. The term "personeity" was coined by Samuel Taylor Coleridge, while Horace Bushnell spoke of the divine "impersonations." See Coleridge's *Aids to Reflection*, ed. John Beer (Princeton, N.J.: Princeton University Press, 1993), p. lxxvi; and Bushnell's address, "Concio ad Clerum: A Discourse on the Divinity of Christ" (1848), in *Horace Bushnell*, ed. H. Shelton Smith (New York: Oxford University Press, 1965), 175.

13. In this section I draw on material published in my *Winds of the Spirit*, pp. 249–64. Used by permission of the publisher. The reader is referred to this section ("The Shape of Christ: Revisioning a Theology of Incarnation") for a fuller indication of my approach to christology.

14. See James M. Robinson, "Very Goddess and Very Man: Jesus' Better Self," in Stephen T. Davis, ed., *Encountering Jesus: A Debate on Christology* (Atlanta: John Knox Press, 1988), 115–16. See also Schüssler Fiorenza, *Jesus*, 147–50.

15. Schüssler Fiorenza, *Jesus*, 89–95.

16. Ibid., 139.

17. For the following I rely on Robinson, "Very Goddess and Very Man," 116–21; Johnson, *She Who Is*, 98–100, 156–59, 165–69; Schüssler Fiorenza, *Jesus*, 139–44; Elisabeth Schüssler Fiorenza, *In Memory of Her: A Feminist Theological Reconstruction of Christian Origins* (New York: Crossroad, 1983), 130–40; and Antoinette Clark Wire, "The God of Jesus in the Gospel Sayings Source," in *Reading from This Place*, vol. 1: *Social Location and Biblical Interpretation in the United States*, ed. Fernando F. Segovia and Mary Ann Tolbert (Minneapolis: Fortress Press, 1995), chap. 17.

18. Gabriel Moran discusses some of the similarities between Socrates, Buddha, and Jesus—all great teachers who rebelled against the established teachings of their time and who taught partly by example, since they were aware in different ways of the limitations of teaching. See *Showing How: The Act of Teaching* (Valley Forge, Pa.: Trinity Press International, 1997), 17–20. For this very reason the person of Socrates is linked with his teaching, which for over two millennia has been referred to as the "Socratic method." The skill of the teacher is required to make the method work well, and the teacher's life is lived in accord with his teaching. Hence Kierkegaard is only partly right about the difference between Socrates and Christ.

19. See J. N. D. Kelly, *Early Christian Doctrines,* 95, 115–17, 140, 143–48, 303–17.

20. See John Hick, *The Metaphor of God Incarnate: Christology in a Pluralistic Age* (Louisville, Ky.: Westminster John Knox Press, 1993), esp. 106–11.

21. See Edwards, *Jesus the Wisdom of God,* chap. 2.

22. Douglas F. Ottati, *Jesus Christ and Christian Vision* (Louisville, Ky.: Westminster John Knox Press, 1989, 1996), chaps. 4–5.

23. Ottati cites here C. H. Dodd's article "Jesus as Teacher and Prophet," in *Mysterium Christi: Christological Studies by British and German Theologians,* ed. G. K. A. Bell and Adolf Deissmann (New York and London: Longmans, Green & Co., 1930), 53–55.

24. See essays by Anselm T. Sanon and François Kabasélé in Robert J. Schreiter, ed., *Faces of Jesus in Africa* (Maryknoll, N.Y.: Orbis Books, 1991), chaps. 6, 8.

25. See essays by Seiichi Yagi, Aloysius Pieris, and Jung Young Lee in R. S. Sugirtharajah, ed., *Asian Faces of Jesus* (Maryknoll, N.Y.: Orbis Books, 1993), chaps. 2, 3, 4.

26. M. Thomas Thangaraj, *The Crucified Guru: An Experiment in Cross-Cultural Christology* (Nashville: Abingdon Press, 1994), esp. chaps. 2, 4, 5.

27. Denis Edwards offers a fascinating discussion of Wisdom and cosmic/ecological redemption in *Jesus the Wisdom of God,* chap. 3. The linkage of pedagogy and ecology is an important aspect of the subject that I have decided for reasons of economy of space not to pursue.

28. For a summary of these theories, see Kelly, *Early Christian Doctrines,* 375–77. The mystical or transformational theory associated with Eastern theology (Greek and Russian Orthodoxy) is probably closer to the pedagogical model than the predominant Western doctrines; see the discussion below of John Hick's work.

29. See Paul Ricoeur, "Religion, Atheism, and Faith," in Alasdair MacIntyre and Paul Ricoeur, *The Religious Significance of Atheism* (New York: Columbia University Press, 1969), esp. 60.

30. See Kelly, *Early Christian Doctrines*, 163–69.

31. Ibid., 170–77, 183–85.

32. Ibid., 381–82, 392.

33. Ibid., 393–94.

34. Hick, *The Metaphor of God Incarnate*, chap. 12 (quotations from pp. 130–32).

35. Ibid., chap. 13 (quotation from p. 136). Hick develops this idea more fully in *An Interpretation of Religion: Human Responses to the Transcendent* (New Haven, Conn.: Yale University Press, 1989); see p. 14.

36. *The Metaphor of God Incarnate*, chap. 14.

37. For the analogy applied to education, see G. W. F. Hegel, *Phänomenologie des Geistes*, ed. Johannes Hoffmeister (Hamburg: Felix Meiner Verlag, 1952), 27: "Education, viewed from the side of individuals, consists in their laying hands on this element that is already available, making its inorganic nature organic to themselves [lit., "consuming its inorganic nature," *seine unorganische Natur in sich zehre*] and taking possession of it for themselves" (translation from *G. W. F. Hegel: Theologian of the Spirit*, ed. Peter C. Hodgson [Minneapolis: Fortress Press, 1997], 99). For the analogy applied to the eucharist, see Hegel, *Lectures on the Philosophy of Religion*, vol. 3: *The Consummate Religion*, ed. and trans. Peter C. Hodgson et al. (Berkeley and Los Angeles: University of California Press, 1985), 154 (1821 lecture manuscript): "This aspect [of the eucharist], that of an immediately sensuous partaking, is expressed in the mode of eating and drinking, and this is in fact the only possible form. For, unlike breathing and the relation of skin to air and water, eating and drinking are just this: appropriating something consciously, and indeed on an individualized basis, to oneself as this and only this sensible, singular subject."

38. See Seiichi Yagi, "Christ and Buddha," in *Asian Faces of Jesus*, 32–44. Yagi adopts and modifies Takizawa's theory as set forth in *Buddhism and Christianity: Critical Comments on Hisamatsu's Atheism* (1964).

39. For the following see Karl Rahner, *Hearer of the Word: Laying the Foundation for a Philosophy of Religion*, trans. of the 1st ed. by Joseph Donceel, ed. Andrew Tallon (New York: Continuum, 1994), esp. chaps. 3, 5–6, 14.

40. Alfred North Whitehead, *The Aims of Education and Other Essays* (New York: Free Press, 1967), 39–40.

41. A question that remains unanswered by this study is how the

pedagogy of God's Wisdom mediated through Western culture might be similar to and different from that mediated through other great cultural trajectories. That is an important agenda for future investigation.

42. David H. Kelsey, *To Understand God Truly*, chaps. 3–4; and *Between Athens and Berlin: The Theological Education Debate* (Grand Rapids: Wm. B. Eerdmans Publishing Co., 1993), chap. 1.

43. The former expression is the subtitle of the *Phenomenology of Spirit* (1807), and the latter is the title of the textbook Hegel first published in 1817 to supplement his lectures.

44. David H. Kelsey, in personal correspondence with the author. I am grateful to Professor Kelsey for pressing me on this matter.

45. Rebecca Chopp identifies three forms of knowing appropriate for theological education today: justice, dialogue, and imagination. See *Saving Work: Feminist Practices of Theological Education* (Louisville, Ky.: Westminster John Knox Press, 1995), chap. 5. Martha Nussbaum identifies three capacities essential to the cultivation of humanity today: critical examination of oneself and one's traditions, ability to see oneself bound to all other human beings by ties of recognition and concern, and narrative imagination. See *Cultivating Humanity: A Classical Defense of Reform in Liberal Education* (Cambridge, Mass.: Harvard University Press, 1997), 9–10.

46. Edward Farley, "Paideia as Thinking: Trans-Method Elements in Graduate Theological Education" (unpublished paper prepared for Auburn Center Seminar on the Doctoral Education of Theological Faculties, 1995), 2–8.

47. Charles W. Anderson, *Prescribing the Life of the Mind: An Essay on the Purpose of the University, the Aims of Liberal Education, the Competence of Citizens, and the Cultivation of Practical Reason* (Madison, Wis.: University of Wisconsin Press, 1993), chap. 6.

48. John C. Bean, *Engaging Ideas: The Professor's Guide to Integrating Writing, Critical Thinking, and Active Learning in the Classroom* (San Francisco: Jossey-Bass, 1996), xi–xiii, 2–3, 18.

49. For a fuller elaboration of this point, see my *God in History: Shapes of Freedom* (Nashville: Abingdon Press, 1989), chap. 3; and *Winds of the Spirit*, chap. 9.

50. See bell hooks, *Teaching to Transgress: Education as the Practice of Freedom* (New York: Routledge, 1994), chaps. 10, 13.

51. For the summary that follows see Maria Harris, *Teaching and Religious Imagination*, p. xv and chaps. 1–6. Her most recent book is coauthored with Gabriel Moran, *Reshaping Religious Education: Conversations on Contemporary Practice* (Louisville, Ky.: Westminster John Knox Press, 1998).

52. Bernard E. Meland, *Higher Education and the Human Spirit* (Chicago: University of Chicago Press, 1953), 13.

53. Ibid., chap. 5.

54. This phrase succinctly expresses George Eliot's aesthetic and religious sensibility, which in chapter 17 of *Adam Bede* (1859; Harmondsworth, Middlesex: Penguin Books, 1980, pp. 223–24) she epitomizes in terms of the exquisite realism of Dutch painting, a realism that nonetheless sees beauty in the midst of the commonplace and the "divine mystery" (p. 81) in the joys and sorrows of human beings. To a friend George Eliot wrote that all of the scientific "explanations of processes by which things came to be produce a feeble impression compared with the mystery that lies under the processes" (to Barbara Bodichon, 5 December 1860). See *The George Eliot Letters*, ed. Gordon S. Haight, vol. 3 (New Haven, Conn.: Yale University Press, 1954), 227. This mystery has to do with the power by which human beings are formed, educated, and reoriented—precisely from self-centeredness to reality-centeredness. In a future work I hope to develop this interpretation and to show that George Eliot's novels are *Bildungsromane* with profound pedagogical, ethical, religious, even theological implications.

55. Samuel Taylor Coleridge, "Apologia Pro Vita Sua" (1800): "The poet in his lone yet genial hour / Gives to his eyes a magnifying power: / Or rather he emancipates his eyes / From the black shapeless accidents of size— / In unctuous cones of kindling coal, / Or smoke upwreathing from the pipe's trim bole, / His gifted ken can see / Phantoms of sublimity." (From *The Complete Poetical Works of Samuel Taylor Coleridge*, ed. E. H. Coleridge [Oxford: Clarendon Press, 1912]. Reprinted by permission of Oxford University Press.)

56. See Anderson, *Prescribing the Life of the Mind*, chap. 6.

57. Nussbaum, *Cultivating Humanity*, 29–35, 294–300. Following the ancient philosopher Seneca, she enunciates four principles of a liberal education: it is for every human being; it should be suited to the circumstance and context of students; it should be pluralistic, concerned with a variety of different norms and traditions; and it must ensure that "great books" do not become unquestioned authorities. Even in vocational programs Nussbaum found elements of liberal education present (see p. 5).

58. See *Cultivating Humanity*, chaps. 4–7. I discuss some of these issues in a paper, "Liberal Theology and Transformative Pedagogy," prepared for a conference on the future of liberal theology in York, England, March 1999. The papers will be published by T. & T. Clark.

59. Craig Dykstra, "Reconceiving Practice," in Wheeler and Farley, eds., *Shifting Boundaries*, chap. 2.
60. Don S. Browning, "Toward a Fundamental and Strategic Practical Theology," in *Shifting Boundaries*, chap. 10.
61. Chopp, *Saving Work: Feminist Practices of Theological Education*, chap. 4, esp. pp. 76–78, 86. My use of the concept of "human flourishing" is indebted to Chopp.
62. See *God in History*, chap. 4; and *Winds of the Spirit*, chap. 18.
63. I am indebted to Edward Farley for this suggestion.

5. Conclusion: Paideia in Higher Education Today

1. Martha C. Nussbaum, *Cultivating Humanity: A Classical Defense of Reform in Liberal Education* (Cambridge, Mass.: Harvard University Press, 1997), 30–35, 293–300.
2. Ibid., 2–3. Nussbaum based her conclusions on in-depth studies of teaching at six quite different institutions across the country: St. Lawrence University in upstate New York, University of California at Riverside, University of Nevada at Reno, Bentley College in Waltham, Massachusetts, the University of Chicago Law School, Brigham Young University. She made briefer studies at two religiously affiliated schools, University of Notre Dame and Belmont University in Nashville; and at two predominantly African American colleges, Morehouse and Spelman in Atlanta.
3. Bruce Wilshire, *The Moral Collapse of the University: Professionalism, Purity, and Alienation* (Albany, N.Y.: State University of New York Press, 1990), xix–xxv. Wilshire examines alienation in chap. 1, professionalization in chaps. 3–4, and purification rituals in chaps. 6–8. In chap. 5 he considers the effect of professionalization on the field of philosophy, which, he argues, has become preoccupied with expertness in language and arguments and has lost interest in questions of truth and goodness.
4. Ibid., chaps. 11–12. By the "Neolithic circle," he is thinking of Stonehenge and other great circular ruins in Britain and Ireland. A similar image would be the circular councils of Native American tribes.
5. Charles W. Anderson, *Prescribing the Life of the Mind: An Essay on the Purpose of the University, the Aims of Liberal Education, the Competence of Citizens, and the Cultivation of Practical Reason* (Madison, Wis.: University of Wisconsin Press, 1993), viii–xi.
6. Ibid., chaps. 1–2.
7. Ibid., chaps. 1, 6.
8. Ibid., 88–89.

9. Ibid., chap. 7. That the list should culminate in practical philosophy is not surprising, coming as it does from a political scientist/philosopher.

10. See ibid., 91–92, 117–20 (see above, chap. 3, sec. 1).

11. Denise Lardner Carmody, *Organizing a Christian Mind: A Theology of Higher Education* (Valley Forge, Pa.: Trinity Press International, 1996), 25–27. Two earlier works elaborate in a helpful way, principally from a Protestant perspective, the connection between liberal education and the study of religion: Howard Lowry, *The Mind's Adventure: Religion and Higher Education* (Philadelphia: Westminster Press, 1950), esp. chaps. 3–4; and Christian Gauss, ed., *The Teaching of Religion in American Higher Education* (New York: Ronald Press, 1951). During the past decade a host of books on this subject has been published: Frank Reynolds and Sheryl Burkhalter, eds., *Beyond the Classics? Essays in Religious Studies and Liberal Education* (Atlanta: Scholars Press, 1990); George M. Marsden, *The Soul of the American University: From Protestant Establishment to Established Nonbelief* (New York: Oxford University Press, 1994); George M. Marsden and Bradley J. Longfield, eds., *The Secularization of the Academy* (New York: Oxford University Press, 1992); Philip Gleason, *Contending with Modernity: Catholic Higher Education in the Twentieth Century* (New York: Oxford University Press, 1995); Douglas Sloan, *Faith and Knowledge: Mainline Protestantism and American Higher Education* (Louisville, Ky.: Westminster John Knox Press, 1994); Mark R. Schwehn, *Exiles from Eden: Religion and the Academic Vocation in America* (New York: Oxford University Press, 1993); Merrimon Cunninggim, *Uneasy Partners: The College and the Church* (Nashville: Abingdon Press, 1994); Conrad Cherry, *Hurrying Toward Zion: Universities, Divinity Schools, and American Protestantism* (Bloomington, Ind.: Indiana University Press, 1995). A number of these works are reviewed by Daniel Sack, "Struggling for the Soul of the American University: Studies on Religion and Higher Education," in *Religious Studies Review* 23 (Jan. 1997): 35–39. Several recent issues of *The Journal of the American Academy of Religion* have been devoted to this topic, notably the fall 1997 issue (vol. 65:4), which contains papers presented at an AAR-sponsored consultation on "Teaching and Learning in Religion and Theology."

12. Carmody, *Organizing a Christian Mind*, 62–64, 88–92, 121–23.

13. Of the six courses, three of an introductory nature would be specifically required and the remaining three would be electives. The same pattern would hold in the other major zones of reality. Of a baccalaureate curriculum of 40 courses, 24, or 60 percent,

would be distributed equally across the four zones. The remaining 16 courses would consist of a major and additional electives. The six courses in religion would represent 15 percent of a student's total college program.

14. Ibid., chap. 4, quotation from p. 158.

15. Ibid., 158–61, 180–84. Carmody's theological orientation is especially influenced by Bernard Lonergan, Karl Rahner, and Eric Voegelin. This way of paraphrasing Irenaeus's statement, from *Against Heresies* 4.20.7, is suggested by Elizabeth A. Johnson, *She Who Is: The Mystery of God in Feminist Theological Discourse* (New York: Crossroad, 1992), 14.

16. Nussbaum, *Cultivating Humanity*, chap. 8.

17. Edward Farley, *The Fragility of Knowledge: Theological Education in the Church and the University* (Philadelphia: Fortress Press, 1988), 178–83 (quotation from 180).

18. See ibid., 120, 124.

19. For what follows, see Farley, chap. 4 ("The Place of Theology in the Study of Religion"); and Francis Schüssler Fiorenza, "Theological and Religious Studies: The Contest of the Faculties," in Barbara G. Wheeler and Edward Farley, eds., *Shifting Boundaries: Contextual Approaches to the Structure of Theological Education* (Louisville, Ky.: Westminster John Knox Press, 1991), 119–49.

20. David F. Ford, "Theology and Religious Studies at the Turn of the Millennium: Reconceiving the Field," *Teaching Theology and Religion* 1:1 (Feb. 1998): 4–12.

21. See below, n. 23.

22. I have benefited greatly from the discussions of this group and from two papers by Edward Farley: "Rethinking Graduate Theological Education," and "Paideia as Thinking: Trans-Method Elements in Graduate Theological Education."

23. For what follows, see David H. Kelsey, *To Understand God Truly: What's Theological about a Theological School* (Louisville, Ky.: Westminster John Knox Press, 1992), esp. chaps. 5, 8–10. Another recent work that has been helpful for me is Rebecca S. Chopp's *Saving Work: Feminist Practices of Theological Education* (Louisville, Ky.: Westminster John Knox Press, 1995), esp. chaps. 4–5 (see above, chap. 4, note 61). Both Kelsey and Chopp rely on Edward Farley's earlier book *Theologia: The Fragmentation and Unity of Theological Education* (Philadelphia: Fortress Press, 1983), which more than any other work launched the current phase of discussion.

24. John Cobb argues that a rejection of the disciplinary organization of knowledge does not entail a rejection of disciplined thinking and specialization. Rather, the division of responsibility in a theo-

logical school should not be according to separate subject matters abstracted from the world, but according to practical goals and the needs of communities of faith. His and Joseph Hough's emphasis on congregationally oriented theological education has had some influence on Kelsey. See Cobb's essay, "Theology against the Disciplines," in *Shifting Boundaries*, chap. 8; and Joseph C. Hough, Jr., and John B. Cobb, Jr., *Christian Identity and Theological Education* (Chico, Calif.: Scholars Press, 1985), which is discussed by Kelsey in *Between Athens and Berlin: The Theological Education Debate* (Grand Rapids: Wm. B. Eerdmans Publishing Co., 1993), 157–73.

25. Kelsey, *To Understand God Truly*, 245, 248.

26. See Kelsey, *Between Athens and Berlin*, 77–81. The reference is to H. Richard Niebuhr's *The Purpose of the Church and Its Ministry: Reflections on the Aims of Theological Education* (New York: Harper & Row, 1956), esp. 107–34.

27. Irenaeus, *Against Heresies* 4.20.7. See above, n. 15.

INDEX